THE Breakup BAND AID

Sarah Melland

Copyright © 2017 Sarah Melland

Published by: Ripe Melland Media

All rights reserved. No part of this publication may be reproduced, stored in a retrieval system, or transmitted, in any form or by any means, electronic, mechanical, photocopying, recording, or otherwise, without the prior written permission of the publisher.

ISBN: (paperback) 9780692049457

ISBN: (ebook) 9780692049457

Front Cover Design by: Sara Mason
www.saramason.wordpress.com

DEDICATED TO MY EX-BOYFRIENDS

You taught me to love, to hate, to stalk and to profit from it.
For that, I thank you.

CONTENTS

How to Use This Guidebook...I
Introduction...IV

Step 1: Admit You Are Powerless Over Your Ex   1
Step 2: Get Rid of Everything Reminding You of Your Ex   5
Step 3: Get a Sponsor. We Know You're Being a Trainwreck   11
Step 4: Make a List of What a Spectacular Catch You Are   16
Step 5: Admit What You Did Wrong in the Relationship   20
Step 6: Don't Contact or Stalk Your Ex for 60 Days   25
Step 7: Quit Your Bad Habits   29
Step 8: List People You Have Harmed While Being a Trainwreck   32
Step 9: Apologize to Them   34
Step 10: No One Likes a Backslider   37
Step 11: Last-Ditch Effort   40
Step 12: Wake Up and Smell the Coffee   44

Quick Reference Guide...47
Don't Ever Do These Things, Psycho!...................................48
Do These Instead..56
Travel Bucket List...62
Top 10 Lists..67
Amazing Comfort Foods..90
Most Used Breakup Lines..94
Comebacks for When Your Ex Says It's Over......................99
How to Make Your Ex Jealous...103
More Dumb Breakup Stories So You Don't Have to..........105

HOW TO USE THIS GUIDEBOOK

This book is meant to be a quick read on your lunch break. If you are unsure of something, skim the "Step By Step" part. If you want to laugh and get your mind off the breakup, read "How NOT To Use This Step". This part will show you exactly how not to use that step. I cannot guarantee 100% satisfaction. Ultimately, it is up to you whether you want to let that scammer go or if you want to live a miserable life thinking about them.

GETTING STARTED

Break up? Check. Stop crying for one second. Ask yourself, was your ex indisputably that great? The answer is no. If you were 100% truly satisfied, you wouldn't have broken up. If you were really as in love as you thought, you would have been able to work it out through thick and thin, rain or shine, and all the other BS. You are alone right now, and that is the only reason you feel you were so in love with them. Get a cat, or a dog, or a hamster, or fidget gadget, and a vibrator. Not necessarily in that order.

Chances are, you are the breakee. You are devastated. You are probably asking yourself, "Why?" Don't. It's not worth the effort or time. Breakups happen every seven seconds. (That's not true, don't fact check me.)

You should stop caring. Clearly, the other person didn't care enough about you. STOP OBSESSING! I mean stop. I mean right now. The way you get started is to STOP!

RELATIONSHIPAHOLICS

Now, if you are "one of those" who jump from one relationship to the next (you know who you are), I am here to tell you it doesn't work. You must not have been that vulnerably invested in the first place. It's a joke. It's annoying for your friends when you fall in love again after two dates. Give me a break. NO! You are not in love; you want to be because you are in such a hurry to get married. A lot of curse words come to mind right now about the way you handle a breakup. I should genuinely feel sorry for you. You will never learn what you did wrong in the last relationship and correct it in the next one. You will continuously bounce around, which is a sad way to live life.

EXAHOLICS

The next character accurately describes how I am; way out in left field batting about a .220. (No idea if that is the correct baseball term. You will quickly learn I don't check my facts.)

Another way you should not handle a breakup is: recklessly. Are you "one of those" psychos slashing tires, stalking your ex, and sobbing all the time? What person in their right mind would ever want to date you???? Yeah, it's pathetic. I mean it's incontestably, disgustingly pathetic. I know you can't help it. Even I can't. I did it. It was not pretty. We all have different ways to cope. This is the most self-destructive. You have no chance of ever getting your ex back after acting as if you should be in a mental institution.

Some people go through a breakup normally. This book is NOT for them. I don't need to spend time talking about how lucky they are to be somewhat sane, or frankly developed without a heart. What is normal, though? Honestly...

THE Breakup BAND AID

This book only helps people who have had their hearts crushed into small bits, put in a coffee grinder, and sipped by some idiot at Starbucks.

INTRODUCTION

My name is Sarah Marie Melland. I have a Ph.D. from The Self-Deprecating Academy. I am not an expert in this field, but I did a lot of research; never acting on what it said. I am living proof the advice probably would have worked better if I had listened to it. That is why I am telling you to just do my damn experiment.

It might hurt like hell, but you won't get them back calling them every two minutes. If you broke up, there was a reason. Get on with your life and stop living in the past. There is nothing you can do to change it now. Getting over a breakup is like a Band-Aid, just yank it off with force!

His name was Eric. He was a bouncer at the most popular bar in our college town. The first time I met him I knew something special was going to happen with him. I knew he was the guy I was going to lose my V card to… soberly. When he asked me to take my (fake) ID out, it was game on. No one turns this twenty-year-old down when she needs a drink! How was I going to conquer this enormous feat on my hands of trying to get into the best bar on the strip? I walked ten more feet and entered through another door. While in the bar, I kept staring at him. I could tell he was a dork trying to be cool. He was lacking in that department, but he was tall with luscious lips, a bangin' body, and he dressed OK. He was a project waiting for my transformation.

The next time I went to the bar, I noticed he was working the door. I slammed the door in his face and walked to the other side. I could tell this was going to be the start of a beautiful relationship.

For months I ignored him. Finally, in the middle of winter, when I was a bit tipsy, I went up to him and asked if he was cold. He said he was fine, but I could tell he was shivering. I offered him my gray zip-up hoodie. Yeah, I volunteered my stupid sweatshirt to a 6'4" football-player. Still no vibe from him. I asked his name. He said, "Eric," while looking straight ahead, not even glancing at my intense hazel eyes.

The next night (because I'm a raging… ahem… college student), he was out. Like actually out. He wore an ironed, white button up. He looked HOT. Instead of a worn-in baseball cap, he had his hair gelled. To my surprise, he grabbed me and said he was heading over to the bar where he worked. Apparently, in my drunken stupor, I was an excellent talker, and we exchanged numbers.

We began dating. Eric ended up being the most amazing man I had ever met. On our second date, he made me homemade chicken noodle soup because I was sick. We moved fast in our relationship. It was intense. There was no in-between ground. We either absolutely adored each other and wanted to spend the rest of our lives together on a remote island never to be bothered by anyone else, or I wanted to claw his face off and trip him.

Our relationship was on the brink of destruction. We were fighting every other day about superfluous issues, but it warranted a yell or two. My girlfriends were pushing me to dump him because they were single. I listened to them even though I knew Eric and I loved each other. He agreed. He actually agreed. Over a text message, coward! Yes, I broke up with him in a text message, and he agreed. No talking. Nothing. I immediately called him. He said he couldn't take the fighting anymore. I hung up the phone and drove over to that duck-lips' house. I went into his room and threw a vase he gave me at his head. He dodged it. All he could say was sorry.

I walked out, got into my car and bawled for extreme lengths of time. I couldn't even start the car. I got home and was retching. I cried through the night. He wasn't next to me, where he'd been for the last year. I didn't know where to sleep. I was hopelessly lost without him. I wanted him to hold me even though I hate cuddling.

THE Breakup BAND AID

I went to my final exam in the morning with no sleep. The professor asked me if I was OK since I couldn't stop sobbing. I said, "No, now give me the worthless test."

I wanted to die. I had never ever felt this abandoned in my life. I knew I needed to sleep with someone hotter than him. Fast.

As I conclude, this is where the "do as I say, not as I do" part comes into play. You will learn how NOT to become a psycho. Have a super day!

STEP 1:
Admit You Are Powerless Over Your Ex

WHAT THE HELL DOES THAT MEAN?

You are a nervous breakdown waiting to happen. You can't even function properly. Every word out of your vacuous mouth is your ex's name. You keep replaying every idiosyncratic part of your relationship in your head until it hurts too much to think, then you take a nap to escape the depression. Yes, admitting you have a problem is the first step. How simple is that? No, it's not, because your dumbass thinks you two can still get back together.

You have called your ex 50 times saying you are sorry and you will change on their voicemail. There is no more room on the voicemail, so you text the same exact thing.

You bring over a care package with tranquil music, candles, condoms and a Caramello candy bar (his favorite) thinking you can reconcile. His roommate answers the door with an eye roll. You walk into his room. He thanks you for the package and shuts the door in your face. You scream, pounding on his door saying how selfish and what an inconsiderate prick he is. I walk out bawling, oops, I meant you walk out bawling.

You have now hit rock bottom. Most exaholics have lost their power to think logically. Our willpower has become non-existent and we know no humility. Myself, obviously, included.

Another sad part is you probably called in sick to work so you could stay home and cry. You try to clean your house spotless to get your mind off the breakup. You can't eat right now. Food makes you want to hurl. Even your stomach is upset with the douchebag that broke your heart. Or you're a comfort eater and need something to fill the void in your life of not having a significant other. Let the binge begin.

Have you noticed your psychotic triumphs have been epic failures? Have people walked away from you because they sensed you were crazy? Have you gotten your ex back yet? If you are even reading these questions and pondering them, yep, you have a problem. Hitting rock bottom isn't so terrible, you have nowhere else to go but up:) Yes, I did a smiley face as punctuation in a book:) I might do it every time:) It will make you at least crack a half-smile:) Maybe:)

Listen, your breakup is not horrifically bad. I take that back. It is egregious, only if you are in the LA area. All the guys are assholes. You are better off alone. Struggling actors and musicians all are feces on the bottom of your stiletto. They think they are the cream of the crop because LA is the land of opportunity. Where was I going with this? I don't know. Don't be lame and waste your time crying. Admit you have a problem.

STEP BY STEP INSTRUCTIONS

1. You are powerless over your ex. Say out loud: "I am powerless over my ex."
2. Your life has become unmanageable since the breakup. Say that too, out loud please so you can hear how foolish you actually sound. To think your total well-being seems to have ended since someone broke up with you, seriously?
3. Free your mind and meditate. If you don't believe in meditation then basically stop thinking about them. Focus on

your passion. If you don't have a passion, look at the "Do These Instead" part for ideas.
4. Stop crying.
5. Go back to work.
6. Eat what you would typically eat on any given day. Stick to a 1200 calorie meal plan and exercise regimen.
7. Take up your whole bed and own it. No one should be sleeping there but you or a random if you deem necessary. (Not too much though, some of them might be bad or have a smaller penis which could make you even more depressed.)
8. Do whatever you want today because you can.
9. Stop worrying if you are going to see them or not. It's not worth it. You should always look your best. You don't want people pointing at you and making faces.
10. There are ten of these? Umm…read the next chapter for more insightful instructions.

HELPFUL TIPS

1. Stop watching love stories for a few weeks. We all know real life doesn't happen as a fairytale.
2. Don't hang out with people who are in relationships. It will only make you feel shitty you are not in one.
3. Go for a walk if you sense a torrential amount of water coming from your eyes. You don't want people to see you cry in public. How embarrassing would that be?
4. Clean out your car. No one does that enough.
5. Go to a restaurant alone. No, I take it back, don't. Bad idea, Sarah!

HOW Not TO USE THIS STEP

Here is the first "How NOT to Use This Step". Mind you, NEVER EVER, I mean fucking EVER pull this shit at home. These are my own experiences and mine alone. Learn from my mistakes and see how much they don't pay.

Well, here goes. I was in the denial stage of my breakup. I mean I was incredibly subdued, down in a hole. I managed to lose seven pounds in seven days because I never ate. However, it was probably water weight from all the tears I shed.

How did I figure out I was powerless over my ex? How did I know I hit rock bottom? Then went ten feet farther? Here's how. I was finally ready to have a night with the girls and forget about this bellend.

I live in a pretty small college town where everybody knows everyone. I bought a new shirt with "Single and Loving It" across the front. The back side read "Back on the Market". Classy, I know. I exude class. Yes, I absolutely wore this magnificent work of art to his bar. The bar where everyone knows me, the one where everyone knows him. Can we spell desperation? I am so glad I was completely plastered; I would have felt moronic if I was sober.

One of his best friends came up to me, asked me why was I broadcasting this and said I should leave because I was annoying. Awesome. What did I do? I stayed, made out with a random right in front of him, probably flashed my tits to some other patrons, and puked in the bathroom. Again, I exude class. Why would he ever want me back? Why would any guy want me like this?

No, unfortunately, it's not over. I went home and added my ex as a friend on Facebook.

Please for the love of God, DON'T buy a breakup shirt! It might seem funny at the time, but you look like an asshole.

The long and the short of it, admit your ex is never coming back. It's so much simpler than going through all the humiliation, in spite of the fact you don't remember any of it.

STEP 2:
Get Rid of Everything Reminding You of Your Ex

WHAT THE HELL DOES THAT MEAN?

I want to be somewhat of a caring person to you during this challenging time, but do you know me? That's just not going to help. I will be a bitch, scream at you in this step until you cry and want to leave. Rest assured, I will not stop. I will be so damn annoying that you will get frustrated out of anger, and throw this book at the wall.

Get rid of EVERYTHING that reminds you of your ex. I don't care if you went to your high school prom and won king and queen together. Get rid of that photo! It's probably in your yearbook anyway. I am not asking you to throw your yearbook away. You can thank me for that gimme.

This step makes everything else go a lot smoother. It might be the hardest step. No, I take it back, the one where you can't stalk is, but this one is equally important.

Please clean out everything. I don't want to repeat myself. It will make your life so much more comfortable in the long run. If you honestly want to save a photo of you two kissing, that's your business, but remember you are always going to look at the pleasant times, not however many times the dickhole screwed you over. Do you honestly want the good memories lingering around? Whenever you are depressed, you are going to look at a picture and make yourself fall into a deeper depression. How embarrassing would it be if you started dating someone and they found that box of memories? They would think you are a freak and dump you. Not good. Not good at all.

If you are a little short on cash, getting rid of their gifts is a fantastic way to earn an extra buck. There are a million avenues to choose from. There are the obvious easy money makers: eBay, Craigslist, garage sales, second-hand shops. Now, more and more people are heading over to NeverLikedItAnyway.com. It is a great way to pour your heart out to complete strangers and explain why you want to get rid of your ex's crap. They have amazing deals on half-used engagement rings. I highly recommend checking this website out if you are in need of a bargain.

If it is during the fall and you live in the Midwest, have a bonfire barbeque with a bunch of your friends. Make a fun night of it, throw everything into the pit and reminisce about how much those crusty capons suck. It will be a letting go ceremony as you cremate your broken relationship.

Goodwill and Salvation Army are other suitable places to do the drop-off. They even come out to your car and grab that junk so fast there is no turning back. If you do these or second-hand shops, I highly recommend you clean out your closet too, and buy yourself a fresh new wardrobe. I hate putting Instagram pictures up that have me wearing an outfit I have already worn in a previous post and so should you.

Please stop clinging to what used to be. It will never be again. Don't go psych ward seven thirty carrying your ex's first condom from when you lost your virginity. Throw it away already. It's weird and creepy.

Other weird and creepy things that need to go: flowers, cards, a piece of paper they wrote a random note on, their favorite beverage, a strand of their hair, their razor, their toothbrush you use to pretend you are still kissing their saliva, their used sweaty sock, fingernail clippings reminding you how their toes used to scratch you. I'm going to hope you get my point. I don't want to go any further as I have a terrible gag reflex.

THE Breakup BAND AID
STEP BY STEP INSTRUCTIONS

1. Get a garbage bag.
2. Trash your ex's t-shirt. Stop smelling it.
3. Take down the shrine.
4. THROW THAT SHIT AWAY NOW! I AM SERIOUS!
5. Now gather up everything. I mean everything reminding you of your ex. A toothbrush, maybe even a lamp? I don't care, throw it away. Yes, even the fucking CD mix you made after the breakup to cry yourself to sleep. (Guilty.) I know you have a Spotify playlist; trash it.
6. Make sure you grab everything. I mean EVERYTHING so a few days down the road you don't find his cum Kleenexes underneath your mattress and start sobbing. (Another true story that, thank God, I didn't experience.)
7. If you had a pet together, then I don't know what the hell you are going to do. If, at all possible, make them take sole custody, or keep the pet out of spite. If you have a kid together, play nice, but don't give them the time of day. The section "How to Make Your Ex Jealous" has more helpful tips since you are going to have to see them from time to time.
8. Clean out your fridge.
9. Now dump all that crap into the bag full of your ex's paraphernalia.
10. Throw it in the garbage can outside. Mission accomplished.

HELPFUL TIPS

1. Think of it as spring cleaning. Think of it as getting rid of the clutter. Your mind will be at peace. You will be free.
2. Whistle while you work.
3. I mean, honestly, who wants dead, dried flowers?
4. Rip it off like a Band-Aid. (That might actually be my favorite saying, along with swearing.) A Band-Aid, to me, represents a patch on a temporary wound like a breakup is temporary. When your wound heals, you take off the Band-Aid and have a fresh start to a new beginning.

5. Don't forget to look under your bed. You might be surprised what you find under there. I found tumbleweeds of my hair. I guess you should always vacuum under your bed if you have hardwood floors.

HOW Not TO USE THIS STEP

I don't know how you can misread this step or do it wrong, but I am sure I can find an example of how I was able to. Mind you, this was before I made up these steps and realized I had a problem. It took me three years to get over Eric. No self-help books worked. I bought every single one of them. I'm praying this helps you for the mere fact that I don't want anybody to end up like me.

I had a box full of utter rubbish. There were three dried roses from when he left me a card on my bed while we were fighting. (See how sad and pathetic it is? I actually know what they were for.) Then, of course, there were pictures. I will name them, so you never end up as miserable and lethargic as I was.

1. 3 photos his mom gave me of his high school graduation.
2. A picture of us kissing.
3. One of us smiling while he was working.

The love letters need to go. The first card he ever gave me. The second card was when we got into a terrible fight because I said he didn't care for me as much as I cared for him. It was extremely sentimental. I had to keep it. I read it over and over again because I finally felt loved. The last one was a Valentine's Day card. The other was a "Let's Not Break Up" card. Oh, I almost forgot, he wrote me a POEM!

> *I think about you when the sun comes up.*
> *I think about you when the sun goes down.*
> *But the worst part is…*
> *I think about you when the sun isn't even around.*

When we broke up, I read these stupid lies over and over and over and over again. I tried to convince myself it was not over. How can it

THE Breakup BAND AID

be kaput when the words on the page said how much he loved me? De-fucking-lusional. Don't believe everything you read.

Ready for the asinine part? I don't think you are. After we broke up, I moved and carried the box of keepsakes with me. I moved again, but this time I wanted to get over him, so I decided to tape the box up. Yes, I taped it up with masking tape. MASKING TAPE! I just taped the corners. One day when I was feeling lonely, I opened it up with scissors, read the lies and cried. Then, read the letters to a new friend who didn't know my breakup story yet. Do I sound pathetic yet? Sadly, the story doesn't end there…

I moved to my next house and thought, "You know what? I am going to tape the fucker up so much I can never get into it." This time, I used a whole roll of masking tape. This time, I took it to another level. I decided I was going to store it at my mom's house so I wouldn't have to look at it every day. I don't know if it can get much worse.

Two years later I was about to move to California, and my Grand Am was packed full of my belongings. I was going to start fresh, buy everything new, and get rid of all my old clothes. I even had to get rid of all my condoms. Then, there was "The Box". The kiss of death. It almost makes me teary-eyed talking about it. No, it doesn't, it wasn't that sensational. You will never guess what happened next? I did it! I finally did it!

Unfortunately, I didn't do it. I told my girlfriend I was living with at the time to do what she wanted with "The Box". Her boyfriend took it and threw it out in the garbage bin, right in front of me. Taking all of two seconds. My memories of my ex flashed before my eyes.

That my friend was the end of "The Box". Now if only I could get rid of some of the photos still in my photo album, it would be perfect. Don't be mad. He looks hideous. I mean, a complete dork, so I feel it is OK. When I look at it, I can't believe I was in love with a doofus. Do as I say, not as I do. Let me be an example of what you NEVER want to be during a breakup. I'm pathetic. Don't be pathetic.

Besides "The Box", there are a few hidden things you should know about and get rid of immediately. One day you are going to find these and start to cry or do something spastic. You need to delete your ex's email from your contact list. I didn't think to do this until I got a surprising spam attack and sent him and everyone else in my contact list some good old-fashion internet porn. Coincidently, the girl had my same name and age. How flipping embarrassing! So, delete their email! You could have it happen to you.

Another quick note: don't look at your phone bill and try to figure out their number. How much more pitiful can you become? Oh, trust me, this is only step two. Also, get rid of the upsetting songs on iTunes reminding you of your ex. Even dance hits you remember of the good times. I'm trying not to leave anything out. You will find out why you have to delete the songs in a different chapter. That step is called "Sensory Therapy".

One more thing: Don't buy a random cheap bottle of perfume when you run out. Apparently, it might be your ex's cologne. My roommate didn't believe me when I bought it accidentally. It was a little sample bottle from Playboy. The packaging was purple. No, I didn't smell it, I like the Russian Roulette feeling of not knowing what kind of smell is in the perfectly packaged bottle. I did it one time with Jennifer Lopez's Miami Glo, which smelled delicious. Why not try it again? Am I right? I never knew what cologne he wore. He had a million bottles on the sink. #FAIL

HOW TO DELETE THEIR NUMBER ON THE IPHONE

I have had some girls tell me you can never get rid of a contact number in your iPhone. You are not trying hard enough. It's fairly simple. First, delete the number. Then try to text them, when their name comes up again, you can remove it from recent contacts. After that, go and save the updates on iTunes in your computer. DON'T restore it, update it. If you have any questions, I am sure you can search in Google. You're welcome.

STEP 3:
Get a Sponsor. We Know You're Being a Trainwreck

WHAT THE HELL DOES THAT MEAN?

You get a damn sponsor! Preferably a best friend or sibling who has your best interests at heart. NOT someone who will give your phone back when you say please. NOT someone who will help you in your stalking mission. Someone who will say no. Say NO to the ludicrousness! I mean they really need to be there for you. Maybe even a parent? You are not going to be nice. Your sponsor is not going to be happy. Instead of calling your ex, you will be calling your sponsor 17 times in a row until they answer their flipping phone! Change your sponsor's name in your phone to your ex's.

    The sponsor has to listen to you whether they want to hear your bullshit or not. You need to take control of yourself, but you probably won't. This is why you are going to need someone else to support you through this process. Don't be upset. It happens to the best of us. Don't take this step for granted. You need them whether you like it or not. Inevitably, you will muck up a time or two. I genuinely hope you don't fail at this. I know some people are going to fail and will write a horrible review of this book. Hey, it's not my fault they couldn't follow directions!

Your sponsor, however, is not your housemaid. They are not there to clean up your dirty messes. You might also choose a sponsor who can relate to your heartache, perhaps someone who feels the exact same way as you. You can probably find those people on Craigslist. Or call Jeff the Lonely Guy. I heard he helps with problems. He's lonely too. He'll listen. He only gets 85,000 calls and texts a day, but I'm sure you will get through.

Your sponsor needs to keep you accountable. Have your sponsor report back to me and tell me how you are progressing. You can reach me on Twitter @ohmymelons. I want updates every week.

A sponsor should be a person you can turn to without embarrassment when questions and problems linked to exaholism arise. Another great sponsor would be someone who has already read this book and understands in its entirety. If you find someone who has read this book, know they have impeccable taste, and they will help you achieve optimum perfection.

Only have one sponsor because with too many you could get confused. Plus, not too many people are going to want to be your sponsor. You are annoying when you're drunk.

In AA, which I pulled my ideas from, you can switch sponsors if you find you will see more growth with another. In my opinion, exaholics shouldn't switch sponsors. You might run out of people willing to put up with your whining. Then you would be left alone, which is unacceptable. Switching sponsors could lead you down a treacherous self-destructive path.

Last but not least, a pet, mammal, fish or any non-living organism cannot be your sponsor, even if you think your cat is a superb listener. She has no idea what the hell you are talking about and can't tell you when you are doing a step wrong. Oh yeah, I saw a Nissan commercial say their new car can do that, but I don't think it can, so stick to humans for the time being.

STEP BY STEP INSTRUCTIONS

1. Find someone who is somewhat coherent and can listen to you bitch for hours.
2. Call them.

3. Ask them if they wouldn't mind being your rock for a few weeks or months or whatever seems plausible. Say please. Maybe say a week, so it doesn't sound too invasive. Anybody can stick to a diet for a week. I mean, yeah, not really, but maybe.
4. If the first person says no, then you need to find someone else.
5. If the second person utters no, you need to find better friends or relatives.
6. Finally, once you locate a suitable person willing to take on the responsibility, you need to give them a checklist of tasks.
7. They need to take all forms of communication away from you.
8. If you need some sort of communication because it is the 21st century, make sure to call them instead of your ex. Program your sponsor's number under your ex's name. (Yes, that is repeated, and for good reason!)
9. Make sure they are willing to listen to you bawl for hours on end, then tell you to STFU.
10. Have them do random checks to make sure you aren't doing anything absurd or embarrassing.

HELPFUL TIPS

1. Do NOT abuse or hit your sponsor. They are only trying to help you.
2. Do NOT make them clean up your messes.
3. Make them an appreciative dinner every once in a while to talk about them for a change.
4. Give them a gift certificate to a spa or something along those lines so they can relax when you are a little bit more stable.
5. Do NOT regurgitate on them when you are drunk.

HOW Not TO USE THIS STEP

Friends get super irritated when they have to watch your every move. I found out. They don't like to carry you out of bars and make sure you don't puke in their brand-new car. It does NOT mean they don't love you. It is a code of ethics not to puke in their vehicle. It is not nice. I don't know why I feel this step is the step where your friends have to take care of you when you are drinking. You do dumb things when you are drunk, that you think are okay. In the little world we call reality, they are the stupidest mistakes you could ever make.

I will make a list to best describe what not to do, which I think I am pretty good at since I am a Virgo.

In no particular order:

1. Find a friend who will take your phone away from you for the whole night! NOT one who will hold it while you are at the bar and then give it back when you get home. That is when all the mischief occurs. I told my friend, Shanna, I needed my phone because I was going to my mom's house or some made up story. She gave me my phone back. What did I do? I decided, what better way to get my ex back than to send half-naked pictures of myself in sexy lingerie. Yeah, didn't work out too well. He told me "No," but his friend would like to come over and meet me. I still had the pictures on my phone when I left it somewhere accidentally and never got it back. Moral of the story: Delete the evidence.
2. Find a friend who won't feed your addiction, tell you it is okay to stalk them and let you use their car to do it. You might not be a good driver, and you might smash into your ex's garbage can. I'm just saying...
3. You need a friend who says you look like shit even when you don't so that you won't pursue your ex. I think fibbing is an outstanding quality to have in a friend. If they say, "You look breathtaking," you are more apt to go and try to stalk your ex. They should ask if you have gained a few pounds or say your face looks bloated. Whatever works. I learned no matter how hot you look, your ex is not going to want you back. Don't try. It isn't worth the time or effort. Believe me. I am so damn gorgeous, and it didn't work all 84 times I tried.
4. Your sponsor needs to have physical strength. They need to be able to hold you back when you see your ex kissing another girl. You don't want it to result in you throwing her over a

THE Breakup BAND AID

banister and getting you kicked out of a bar. It never looks appealing. (Unfortunately, my 6'3 250-pound friend, Luke, was not there to hold me back.)

5. A sponsor should not help you make a fake Facebook profile and look up your ex to see if they are miserable without you. One: no one ever puts that their life is miserable on Facebook unless they are trying to drown in their sorrows of self-pity, and need sympathy. Two: most people private their account anyway. It's practically pointless. If you add them as a friend under your fake profile, they will probably not accept you. You would only have a few friends, which looks weird and suspicious. Three: making a name that sounds believable is hard. We came up with Sheena Valsquer. We also made her an ER Doctor in Chicago somewhere. Who wouldn't want to add her? You are probably asking, "Why would you make a fake profile?" If you search your ex under your Facebook profile, you will be in the people they may know section. You don't want to come up as a stalker. Google it. Do it! Google "Why do certain people come up on the People You May Know?" This, of course, is only if you don't have friends in common with your ex, which most of you probably do. Delete your ex and block them so they can never look at you and you can never look at them. Period. End of story.

6. Now, on to Snapchat. You know better than to watch their stories. They can see it. Don't be stupid. Same with Instagram: they can see who viewed their stories.

7. If I knew how Musical.ly worked, I would tell you what not to do. I think it has something to do with singing? So, don't lip sync them a song and send it to them.

8. I also don't know how Pinterest works. I am sure it has something to do with likes. Don't like anything. Or pin anything they pinned. Yes, I have no idea.

9. Block yourself from all social media.

STEP 4:
Make a List of What a Spectacular Catch You Are

WHAT THE HELL DOES THAT MEAN?

You find the true beauty within yourself. If you don't have any outstanding qualities, then make some up. If you have gained a few pounds, stopped styling your hair or putting on makeup, this step will revamp your image. This step will make you feel confident! You were put on this earth for a purpose. The purpose was not to be with someone who doesn't cherish you.

If you have always wanted your hair short, but your ex preferred it long, cut it. You are allowed to be a human being again. Don't be stuck under their control. You need to shine and all the other clichés you see at the end of movies with a happy ending. These don't happen in real life, but pretending is always optimistic.

Note: You shouldn't put sexual qualities on this list. It will make you feel lonely and depressed. You're probably not as good in bed as you think you are.

THE Breakup BAND AID

I guess if you really wanted to plunge into this halfheartedly, you could pretend your whole life is a business. You wouldn't let your business fail, why should you let your meaning of life fail? Wow, I think I am getting too deep. Not good. The book might become boring, and you won't want to finish it.

I feel you have grown a lot since steps one through three and you should be able to handle this step on your own, while I make a mimosa and lie by my apartment's pool.

I decided the reason my relationships fail is that I like to see an end date. That end date happens to be two months. I also decided I should blame my mother for why I am so messed up in the head with men. My father was rarely there, and I don't particularly like old men. My mom is going to read this. Just kidding, love you mom. Loved helping you stalk when I was 10, and you broke his window. Remember that? That was fun. Where was I going with this? We have all been there is my point. We all have our stories. It's OK. You are beautiful and loved. We have our ups and downs, but we will get through them together.

The reason my first relationship failed was because my girlfriends were single and I liked to start drama. Also, I knew I was always going to move out to LA, and I didn't want his annoying ass dragging me down to his nerdiness level.

I have provided you with some of the most heartfelt, genuine examples I could think of, and I suggest you do the same. Keep it 100, folks.

STEP BY STEP INSTRUCTIONS

1. Get a piece of paper.
2. And a pen.
3. Think for about an hour.
4. First, start by describing your positive physical qualities.
5. Then write character traits. Are you funny? Are you a good listener? Are you friendly?
6. If you are having a hard time listing attributes, call a friend.

7. I feel 50 qualities sounds like a good even number. If it's too many then 25 should be sufficient. If it still seems like a lot to you, like I said in the beginning, make stuff up, then try to become those qualities. If you believe, you will become.
8. Now practice those great qualities and recite them in the mirror like Stuart Smalley (SNL).
9. Treat yourself to a new hairdo when you're done listing all your extraordinary attributes. It will make you feel like a brand-new person and confident about yourself again.
10. Buy a new outfit to go along with your new hair. Have a cocktail with your sponsor at a new bar. Or go out of town for the weekend and have a retreat. Any of those options will suffice.

HELPFUL TIPS

1. Do NOT make up unrealistic qualities you will never possess. For example, if you are 5'4 you will never be 5'9.
2. Don't buy self-help books listing generic traits. I find it does you no good and you can't be certain what they mean. For example, "I am a good person." A good person? In what way? How have you been a good person? Those are too hard to read. They get you confused. Confusion is not a good quality to have.
3. To clarify, this step is not to set goals for yourself. Goals will only stress you out and potentially age you faster.
4. If you can't find enough qualities, look in the thesaurus. Use the same word differently. Perfectly acceptable.
5. If you still can't find enough qualities, make up some cool words. That is a quality in itself. Combine two words to make one super word, i.e. *smokin'hot*.

THE Breakup BAND AID

HOW Not TO USE THIS STEP

Qualities should not be listed and directed toward your ex. Qualities are for your own personal use only. Once again, they don't care. Promising qualities to your ex, like you will change, you will be better, you won't be dramatic. It never actually happens. Pretty much ever.

Your new hairdo and outfit do not give you the right to stalk your ex so they can see you are totally better off without them. They will think, "Man, Sarah looks hot, and I still want to bang her, BUT she is a trainwreck and too clingy." Trust me.

You have a hot new look. Don't go whoring yourself out. People are tramps these days. It's not a safe option. Did you know that even though condoms say they are 90% effective for blocking STDs, the correct number is around 15%! Found out from my gynecologist. Basically, you don't know which Bieber gave you gonorrhea, and of course, you aren't going to call them. Chances are you don't have their number, or you are never going to see them again, so who cares?

Remember, this is only the fourth step. You have a long way to go before you are cured and ready to date. You found some good qualities you didn't know existed about yourself. This, however, doesn't mean you are ready to date. You haven't found out the reason you failed at your last relationship yet. If you start dating, you are going to make the same fatuous mistakes you made last time. Plus, you need to find out what you want from yourself before you have a significant other. They are not going to find it for you. Chances are they're still looking to discover themselves. Case in point, you both are doomed to fail unless one of you, preferably both know what you want in life.

Also, just because you think "motherly figure" is a good quality, don't go out and get pregnant. You are not ready to be a mother!

Last but not least, a fun game to play would be trying to make your bad qualities sound like good ones. If you are a messy person, try saying you are laid back instead. I mean, come on, how much better does that sound?

I just realized I didn't tell you a story of what I did wrong. Oh well, there are more in the back of the book. I took a self-help class and realized I am fabulous. Boom! Character trait domination.

STEP 5:
Admit What You Did Wrong in the Relationship

WHAT THE HELL DOES THAT MEAN?

You need to tell a friend, your sponsor, the homeless guy who sits next to the bank, all of the things you did wrong in your last relationship. Even though you don't think they were wrong. They were wrong, and you are too proud to admit it.

You can't be afraid to admit you were wrong. In this step, you should find out a lot about yourself. No one is perfect. There is no way to judge if you are, so stop thinking you can. Everyone is allowed to make mistakes, be judgmental, and cry for no reason every once in a while.

You need to dig down deep and think. It's not a bad thing if you made numerous mistakes in the relationship, as long as you learn from them and work hard not to repeat. If you do them still, then you have to figure out why you keep repeating your missteps. If you cheated, you should go to sexaholics anonymous or a real therapist. You have issues I cannot cure.

THE Breakup BAND AID

Why do people have a hard time admitting they are wrong? Simple: Google "Cognitive Dissonance Theory" and you will have your answer. I don't have time to explain it. It's actually quite dull, but it does make sense.

Another reason to admit you are wrong is you probably are. In my senior yearbook quote I put, "My opinions may have changed, but the fact that I'm right won't." Wow, pretty much sounds like a bitch no one would want to date.

Once you list all the wrongs you did in your relationship, burn it and never look back. You left that shit in your last relationship. Onward and upward!

STEP BY STEP INSTRUCTIONS

1. Find someone willing to listen to you for a few hours, because you might need to relive some painful memories. Find someone to play Devil's Advocate if you can't think of what you did wrong to make your ex dump you.
2. This is going to require you to recall all the fights. Think of it as a learning tool and not a negative. You might realize the fight was not worth it and you blew it with the best person in your life. No matter what you think, the relationship wasn't going to last much longer anyway. Deep down, you wanted to start a fight.
3. Analyze.
4. Psycho-analyze.
5. You might even want to buy a psychology book. I find they are always helpful.
6. If this isn't the first relationship you have sabotaged, then take a look back. Try to notice patterns.
7. When you find a pattern, step back and reflect. In the next relationship, you should wait before you react in a demonic way.
8. Don't lie. You are in the presence of friends who already love you for who you are, despite all your ridiculous flaws.
9. Let it out! Cry when you need a moment. You are allowed to be weak and vulnerable.
10. Dammit, again, with number 10? You get the gist.

HELPFUL TIPS

1. I would make this friend dinner because you are going to depress them.
2. Maybe take a Xanax?
3. Close your blinds.
4. Tissues are always a good option. I find wiping mucus on your shirt is not appropriate.
5. Lay on the couch like you would at a therapist's office.

HOW Not TO USE THIS STEP

This step is not about what THEY did wrong in the relationship. God knows that list could go on forever. This is strictly about YOU and what YOU did wrong in the relationship.

This one is a touchy subject for me. I realized what I did wrong in the relationship and now was ready to fix it. Only it was too late to fix.

I finally grasped that I was causing too much drama in our relationship. I would start fights to tell my friends about because I thought it was cool to have excitement. Don't ask me why, the dumbest mistake I ever made in my life. I was immature and wanted to be on a reality show.

It was two weeks after we broke up, we were back on speaking terms because we were each other's best friends. He came over one night, and I cooked him leftovers. We chatted, cuddled, and everything was perfect. It felt right to be in each other's arms again.

This is where the story gets sad. I was purposely interfering with my own happiness. No jokes here, this is terrible. He told his friends he might consider getting back together with me because he genuinely thought I had changed.

Did I? Absolutely not. I called him the next night at five and asked him to have dinner with me again. He said he was going out with the boys for a friend's birthday (legitimate reason). What do I do? I go ballistic. I start yelling at him about how he never wants to spend time with me and a bunch of other insignificant shit I care not to repeat. So... fucking... unbelievably... stupid.

This is why when you discover what you did wrong, sit and think. If you don't, you are bound to repeat it. History is never good when it repeats itself, and neither are you. You never hear people say, "Look, history is repeating itself," when it's a good thing. No, you don't. Never, because they don't. They don't say that.

OK, OK, I'm making myself look like the complete screwup when he wasn't so innocent either. Here is a great example. When we were together, we planned to go to his cousin's wedding in Jamaica. When we broke up, since he had already paid for it, he said I could still come. Like an idiot, I thought we were totally going to get back together. That was not the case. The delusional state I was in made no difference. Men are pigs. One week before we were about to go on the trip, he decides to start seeing this bitch, who I heard had... play nice, Sarah.

Did I mention she had a stupid name too? Like super stupid, like why would you date someone with the same name as you with an A at the end. Stupid right?

He brings her to our Triple-A baseball team game. He knew my family would be there. I told him. It was the Fourth of July. That's what everyone does in Eau Claire, Wisconsin on the Fourth of July.

She gets wasted while he is talking to my family after the fireworks. Apparently, he "ran" into us. I get it. I have a pretty damn amazingly hilarious family. I would want to hang out with them all the time too. He loved my family. They are rowdy, authentic and lovable. He starts talking to me about when we should meet for the trip. The trip was in two days. I was mad irritated. He paid for the trip, so I wanted to stick it to him by going, that way he couldn't bring some random girl to Jamaica with his family. Oh, and the ticket was in my name. I think that makes it non-transferable, jackass!

I told him to go fuck himself. (Such a juvenile thing to say.) He could take the inebriated piece of trash hovering over his shoulder! If my family wasn't two feet away from me, I would have put the slut in her place. I was finally the bigger person in this situation.

I thought I would be sneaky and say we could take my car to go to the airport, because when she drove by she would wonder why his car was still on the street. Stupid me. He gave his car to his friend that weekend. So, we start out in a fight. This is going to be an awesome four-hour car ride fighting about a skank. He told me I had to pretend we were still together because his parents would be upset that he spent $1000 on me if we weren't.

We weren't leaving for the airport until early the next morning. When we got there, his mother said we had to sleep in separate rooms. His parents kept saying how beautiful I was and about how cute a couple we were that was making me want this nightmare to be over. No matter how bad I wanted to go to Jamaica, this wasn't going to be worth it.

To make a long story short, there was a little hurricane that year named Dennis. We did not make it to Jamaica. We did, however, spend the weekend at a cabin in Wisconsin Dells. We got drunk and had the perfect time. When we got back to our small town, he went back to her. Even though during our weekend of realizations, he said her personality sucks.

What I am saying is don't get your hopes up about anything. Admit your wrongs and move on. It will make the process go quicker. You won't have false expectations about a relationship that is already over. Trust me. TRUST ME.

STEP 6:
Don't Contact or Stalk Your Ex For 60 Days

WHAT THE HELL DOES THAT MEAN?

This step is the hardest one to do, especially if you live in the same town, go to the same college, take the same classes, go to the same bars, and have the same friends. Guess what? You have to do it! It's not as hard as you are making it out to be...once you stop stalking. Have some self-control!

During this period, I suggest you get off all social media. Make your friends unfriend, unfollow, un-whatever your ex. If your ex has Twitter, they are a loser anyway. If they have Myspace, I cannot help you any further. You better not watch their Snapchats, they can see when you watch their stories, same with Instagram. (It's worth repeating.) Also, don't join their Houseparty! I don't feel that app is taking off, but if it is, get rid of it for 60 days.

If you guys happen to go to the same gym, I know you know their schedule. Don't go when they go. Do whatever you need to do to avoid your ex. I understand how punitive gyms can be about canceling your never-used membership and all the early cancellation fees they tack on. Next time I want a gym membership, I'm going to remember, "It's better to be fat."

If you accidentally see your ex, you have to start the 60 days over. You were obviously not doing a good enough job. I am cruel. After 60 days, it will be easier not to think about them. If not, there are six more chapters in this book which is a bonus for you.

Stalkers are lonely people. I know you think social media stalking is harmless. You are passing the time, looking for a little interpersonal communication. Wrong. Knock it off! Stop making yourself miserable!

You are wondering, "Why 60?" It's a psychology term.

STEP BY STEP INSTRUCTIONS

1. You probably know their phone number by heart, but please delete it out of your phone.
2. Put a number close to your ex's back into your phone and memorize it. Maybe you will forget their number.
3. Don't check their social media. Hell, get off social media for the whole 60 days. It will help your communications skills. No one likes to talk to people who are constantly looking at their phone because they think they are important.
4. Obviously, stalking their house and work is out of the question too.
5. Take a walk outside or buy a workout video instead of going to the gym. I recommend "Slim in Six." Tack on two extra weeks of a bonus video and you have your 60 days. My new favorite is "The Brazilian Butt Lift." Both by BeachBody.
6. Find a new hangout. The one you have been going to isn't cool anymore.
7. Don't text them.
8. Don't email them.
9. Don't call them.
10. Last but not least, don't try to run into your ex at their parent's house.

THE Breakup BAND AID

HELPFUL TIPS

1. Take some vitamins. Going out in the sunshine and getting some Vitamin D will make you feel happy. Or get a B-12 cocktail. I heard those are amazing.
2. If you feel the urge to contact your ex, look up funny blogs. Pretty soon you won't remember what you were looking for in the first place.
3. Go to a concert with friends.
4. I find Netflix always has something amusing playing. I am also in love with binge watching Impractical Jokers. Roku finally added the channel app for TruTV.
5. Do something you always wanted to do like bungee jumping or parasailing.

HOW Not TO USE THIS STEP

OK... I am not entirely sure if I have ever completed this step. I guess that is one big "How NOT To". It's hard. I mean really hard. I even moved across the country and still looked at his damn Facebook from time to time. I couldn't help it I only did it when I was lonely. ONLY when I was lonely. Hey, I finally stopped drunk-dialing him after I got a new phone number. Now, how much willpower is that? A lot, that's how much it is.

There is a great deal of effort you have to put into this step. Please don't call your ex incessantly for two hours straight, then text them, and do it all over again until your phone dies. It does not sound cool. Does it sound cool to you? It sure as hell doesn't get on their nerves to have to hit the silent button every two seconds and delete all those damn worthless texts saying "I hate you." Those texts always make them want to pick up the phone. Wrong.

Don't drunk-dial them at three in the morning and call them seventeen times in a row before they answer, especially when you are in different time zones. I have abused this one. The one where the guys are so disgusted, they don't even look me in the face anymore. I only drunk-dialed when I was younger. I mean, I hope I don't do that anymore. My need for sex and men is slowly dwindling in LA. I have found my hand more useful and less stressful.

Here is a doozy. My ex turned me down for sex for the umpteenth time, so what did I do? I write him a sweet Facebook message. I told him I am so glad he turned me down because I realized who he had slept with after me. I said she was repulsive and I know for a fact she had some sort of STD. (Again, always guessing, but not really.) I feel like it was five paragraphs longer though. I was drunk at three a.m., what's new with you?

On the other side of the bipolar spectrum: I would then write that I was still completely in love with him. He is going to make some girl very happy and what a great guy he is blah blah blah blah blah blah. I wish I could smash things.

How about this one for you? How about joining the same gym he goes to after you broke up? In my defense, I am pretty sure that was the only gym we had in town besides the YMCA.

You know what else you shouldn't do? Drive by their house early in the morning to see if their car is there. It will make you excruciatingly depressed when it's not.

Another NOT smart thing to do is go to their work where they bartend, order a drink every five seconds, and not tip. Probably another good idea is not to throw their co-workers over the banister and get kicked out of the bar.

Oh, and also, DO NOT go to his graduation party uninvited. Apparently, that's frowned upon.

STEP 7:
Quit Your Bad Habits

WHAT THE HELL DOES THAT MEAN?

Figure out what bad habits you have and stop doing them. I am talking about bad habits in general, not just in relationships. We already covered bad habits in relationships or at least what went wrong. This is the part where you have to fix what is wrong with you. What makes you not a lovable person? You have to dig deep into your past. You probably only need to go back as far as kindergarten.

    I have a lot of flaws. One of them is extreme social anxiety. I can never go someplace new without flipping out first. Did I mention I'm pretty much always right? I have an obsession with making lists, but I never follow them. I will for a day, then stop. Then, I start a new list. I stalk people I hated in high school to see if they got fat and how ugly their new husband is. Did I mention I have issues? I make poor decisions when I am drunk. These usually result in me flashing my boobs and making out with some idiot. Mostly, I am too superficial, but that will probably never change, haha. I laughed at myself. Oh dear God, Sarah…

STEP BY STEP INSTRUCTIONS

1. Why not start with the physical? Are you overweight? Did you gain weight during the relationship? Did you let yourself go? Did you stop doing your hair? Makeup? The little things?
2. Think before you speak.
3. Ask yourself, "What could I have done better in contributing to the relationship?"
4. Read Personality for Dummies. If they don't have that, then it will be my next book, since this one is going so well.
5. Were you ever greedy? Nobody likes a taker. Never take the last piece of anything. Etiquette is key.
6. How were you in bed? Spontaneous? If not, you need a sex book from Barnes & Noble. Read Cosmo. Amazon works too. I'm sure that's where you bought my beloved book.
7. Are you uptight or antisocial? If you are, you need to overcome your fears and say yes for once.
8. Are you annoying? If you are, stop.
9. Are you a know-it-all? That can be annoying too. See Step 8.
10. Please don't gossip. Guys like a simple girl with no drama. I found out the hard way. If guys are reading this book, don't gossip.

HELPFUL TIPS

1. Make sure to shave your legs.
2. Wear a sports bra at night to keep your boobs perky. Studies say no. I disagree. I'm 33 and have been doing it since I was postpubescent, and my boobs are perfect.
3. It's best to keep your mouth shut when you first meet a person even if you have the urge to be sarcastic. Apparently, you come across as a bitch.
4. Volunteer your time at the Humane Society. Playing with dogs lowers your blood pressure (I am trying to throw every random fact I have ever heard of into this book. You're welcome.)
5. Don't talk too much, but don't be boring. Life is so hard!

THE Breakup BAND AID

HOW Not TO USE THIS STEP

My boyfriend once said my boobs were too veiny. What the hell does that mean? Excuse me? Let me laser my veins away. They are a DD cup and real. I cannot change that about myself, so I fail as a human being?

I have never had a boyfriend complain about my physical attributes because let's face it, I am gorgeous. If you are not gorgeous, it's OK. (In my opinion, I think everyone can be gorgeous as long as they have self-confidence.) I am sure you have a great personality. I happen to have both, which makes me perfect and hard to find what my shortcomings are.

I am kidding! I am impatient and have a terrible temper. I once screamed at my boyfriend for five minutes about nothing. We got into a lot of fights because I was impatient with him. When we would study together, he was a lot slower reader than I was. It would irritate me.

This is what sucked about us. Well, what sucks about me is a lot of qualities. I went to my ex-boyfriend's graduation party (Here is the story I know you were desperately waiting for.) For some odd reason, I thought it would be a good idea to go up to his parents and make small talk. Yeah, not a good idea. His friends came up to me, told me to get the hell out, and that I was selfish to ruin his graduation party. I informed them that I would leave not because they asked me to, but because I had to get up early in the morning. Which was the truth. I actually did have to get up early and go to work.

I have OCD. The self-diagnosed form anyway. I have routines. I think that is why sometimes it is difficult for me to get my anxiety out of my head. I freak out if I can't do my routines. I get jittery and start screaming at people. I am not going to tell you what my routines are. They are ridiculous, and they really don't even make sense to me. I know a psychologist could cure me, but who has the time or money? I am in massive credit card debt. I don't know why I told you I had OCD. It's somehow correlated with this "How NOT to step". Oh yeah, I am telling you my bad habits. I like to go on tangents. Another bad habit.

STEP 8:
List People You Have Harmed While Being a Trainwreck

WHAT THE HELL DOES THAT MEAN?

This step is pretty self-explanatory, but I mean you did buy a book on how to get over a breakup. Write down all the people who had to put up with your stank. I mean EVERYONE!!!! Your cat, your parents, friends, neighbors, college professors, whomever. Yes, you have to write another effing list. You will be so amazing at making lists by the end of this book. You could make a profession out of it like extreme couponing, but with lists. How exciting!

You need to make a complete list. A list of all the people you put through the trenches. This step is easy. The more I read the next step, the more I realize this has a dual meaning. This means to befriend your exes you have harmed. Ask them what went wrong in the relationship so you get a complete straight answer. This step is only to write their name down. DO NOT write down the name of your current ex you bought this book for. That would completely defeat the purpose.

THE *Breakup* BAND AID
STEP BY STEP INSTRUCTIONS

1. Sit down.
2. Get a pen.
3. Get a piece of paper.
4. Think of everyone you know or have come in contact with after your first breakup.
5. Write their names down.
6. As of right now, that is all you have to do.
7. Think long and hard.
8. I mean EVERYONE!
9. Not just from your first breakup, but all your breakups.
10. DO NOT WRITE DOWN YOUR CURRENT EX's NAME!

HELPFUL TIPS

1. Take a trip down memory lane. Get out your yearbook.
2. A phone book is always helpful. Do they have those anymore?
3. Facebook is good. You better not check your ex's profile, or I will kick your ass!
4. I find a college ruled notebook is always helpful.
5. Pens are better than pencils because you don't have to sharpen them.

HOW Not TO USE THIS STEP

I never did this step. That is how not to do it.

STEP 9:
Apologize to Them

WHAT THE HELL DOES THAT MEAN?

Contact them. I don't know if this step works. I should have been more creative when ripping off Alcoholics Anonymous.

Build back your friendship with them. Tell them you won't be a crazy stalker, and you seriously have changed. Tell them I sent you. Tell them you read this excellent self-help book which changed your whole outlook on life. Say you are a better person because of it and they should buy it too! They don't even need to read it, just having it in their possession will give them good vibes.

No, honestly don't tell them that. I was just trying to boost sales for this book. Telling them you are sorry should be fine.

Any feedback you would like to give me, please tweet me @ohmymelons. Also, follow me on Twitter and Instagram. I heard if you have a lot of followers it's a good thing.

Yes, when I finally registered for Twitter, Sarah Melland was taken. Whatever, @ohmymelons is a way cooler Twitter name anyways. @ohmymelons. Like "OH MY" what did you do? And cantaloupes.

THE Breakup BAND AID

If you have any suggestions on how I can get more followers besides buying them, because it is expensive and they disappear, I am all ears. I already tried. Please tell me @ohmymelons on Twitter. I've tried retweeting people I wanted to follow me, and those bottom feeders tell me I need to follow someone to gain 500 followers. That's an effing lie! I've never gained one follower by doing that. I hate Twitter. It's dead. Everyone does Snapchat and Instagram. Such a self-indulgent world we live in.

And finally, please follow me on all social media @ohmymelons or @yourdatingunexpert. Thank you. Continue reading. There are a few more steps if you are not cured yet.

STEP BY STEP INSTRUCTIONS

1. Look at your list of people.
2. If it is over 100, cut it down to 50, because you probably are going to take a nap.
3. Now cut that down to 20, because let's face it 50 people is daunting.
4. Even 20 is too much. Cut it down to 10.
5. When contacting people, you should go in a random order and not alphabetical.
6. Contact a friend first then an ex.
7. Set up an appointment to meet.
8. DO NOT CONTACT YOUR CURRENT EX!
9. Preferably meet during the day.
10. No drinking should be involved in this meeting.

HELPFUL TIPS

1. Go to a dark place so they can't see when your eyes well up with tears.
2. Shower and "shave"…just in case. (If you don't get why shave is in quotation marks, I cannot help you any further.)
3. I would have a shot of alcohol before you go even though I said not to.

4. Wear a bright fun color. Colorful people always seem happy. You never see people wearing bright colors looking miserable and hating their life.
5. Act content even if you are not. It might trigger something in your brain. Pretending to laugh actually makes me laugh. Try it.

HOW Not TO USE THIS STEP

I bet you can guess what I did? Yep, I slept with the exes. Not the ones I cried over, just ones I remembered had big dicks and were worth my time getting naked for. (Mom, if you are reading this, I know you hate when I talk about men's penis size, but it happens.)

Then I realized why you shouldn't bump nasties after a breakup. They followed me the whole night and totally cock-blocked me! Not cool. One ex was clinging to me like a dryer sheet, and that is when I realized my plan was definitely not as thought out as it could've been. I repeat, DON'T sleep with them. You should pray to God they are married and have children.

If they are still single and look hot, you are allowed one hall pass in this game. It's only logical. No one can quit smoking cold turkey. Sometimes we need help. This is my gift to you. Have sex with an ex, so it doesn't add to your number.

Don't call people you have no interest in talking to, like friends from four years ago you haven't spoken to in three. That's a waste of breath.

Do not reconnect with an old flame. Seriously, don't, if you get dumped by them again, then you have a whole new set of problems.

STEP 10:
No One Likes a Backslider

WHAT THE HELL DOES THAT MEAN?

Make sure you are on the right track and not backsliding. No one likes a backslider. Do activities to keep your mind off being alone. Being by yourself is not the end of the world. You are free to do whatever the hell you want.

Somewhere in this book, I tell you what you should do to discover yourself. Impressed? So am I. Sometimes I care. No, but seriously, I shouldn't take this lightly. AA, OA, NA, SA and all the other great foundations have helped many people overcome addiction. That is why I will be donating $20,000 I make from this book to support them. Hopefully, I make $20,000. I will. Law of Attraction. I know I am joking about how to get over an ex, but I still feel if you do these steps they will help you learn more than you have ever known about yourself, which will in turn help you find your true soulmate.

Please try hobbies you have never done before. Hobbies you have always wanted to do. If you are short on cash like me, Google "Free fun things to do around your area." I give ideas, like I said, somewhere in this book. I don't feel like looking for what I called it right now because I am rushing to finish this chapter before my Packers play.

STEP BY STEP INSTRUCTIONS

1. Look back over the past few weeks and see how much you have accomplished.
2. Look at how beautiful you glow by sticking to a healthy diet and workout regimen.
3. Check off the items on your list.
4. Check off the qualities you definitely have now.
5. You should have confidence too! You sexy mamacita!
6. You should be ready to go out in public.
7. Possibly, I mean possibly, you might be allowed to go on a date at this point. Don't get discouraged. There are still like 4 billion men out there. Most of them are taken or gay, but hey, there is still a shot. And hey, for you guys and girls who are into women, there are 4 billion out there for you too.
8. That is an understatement, but think of it as the glass is half full.
9. Meditate. It calms me down. It's almost as incredible as popping a Xanax.
10. I am getting so lazy.

HELPFUL TIPS

1. It's probably time to get your hair cut again.
2. Stand up straight, stick out your chest. You will look ten pounds thinner.
3. Do volunteer work at an animal shelter. It will make you feel better. Having a dog or cat lowers your blood pressure. I feel I have said that in this book already, but it bears repeating. I like repeating myself.
4. Put your DVDs in alphabetical order. If you don't have DVDs anymore, clean out your pantry.
5. Learn a new language. Duolingo is a cool app and free.

THE *Breakup* BAND AID

HOW *Not* TO USE THIS STEP

Do not take a personal day and go to the beach. I know this step is all about taking care of yourself. All I am saying is please be cautious. I was so upset knowing my ex was dating some ugly chick that I took a personal day off work. My friend Meggan and I thought, man, what a beautiful day, let's go to the beach and drink.

We heard about this place that was amazing. It had waterfalls and a lot of college students go there during the summer. We took for-flipping-ever to get ready. We first went to the mall to find the perfect swimsuit. I was not having luck, got pissed and gave up after two hours. We went home, got a cooler and went to the store for some booze. The beach trip was almost not going to be worth it. It was three, and we still had to drive thirty minutes to get there.

We finally pick up the guys we're going with and all that jazz. We pull into the parking lot and some chick parks right next to us. We get out and then who steps out of her passenger side door? My ex. I am fairly certain God hates me at this point.

I stand there in shock as he spots me. "What is that?" I said. He said, "Stop it." I looked her up, down and laughed. A laugh that meant: I am way better than you, and I can't believe you are trying to date this fuckhead who is still in love with me. That, "If you're having sex with him, he is thinking of me," sort of laugh. I will give her a little credit. She was sort of cute if you like that chubby cheek kind of thing. For the most part, she was pretty unfortunate looking which made me feel good. Take personal inventory. I'm still hot. Check:-)

STEP 11:
Last-Ditch Effort

WHAT THE HELL DOES THAT MEAN?

Sensory Therapy is to stimulate the neurological systems of your brain. It helps condition your brain to remind you of a memory or a smell of a specific memory to go directly to thinking of the idiot and how miserable it was to look at their face.

Apparently, this rarely works according to some studies, but as I said, you are desperate. It is a form of therapy to help autistic children. I did not know that. My mother told me this step is something Dr. Joyce Brothers had said. So, you and I are learning together. Isn't that exciting?

I guess you could also try yoga and breathing techniques which are also forms of Sensory Therapy. Research how to do it because I don't have time to explain it all here. Yoga is too complicated for me. All the weird pose names freak me out. It's like different sex positions. Looking at those pictures give me anxiety because I am not flexible enough to do most of them. This is probably why I should do Yoga. I am too stressed out and don't know how to calm down.

There are two other types of therapy you could also try: Cognitive Processing Therapy and Prolonged Exposure Therapy.

THE Breakup BAND AID

Cognitive Processing Therapy (CPT) helps you by giving a new way to handle distressing thoughts and to gain an understanding of these events. By using the skills learned in this therapy you can understand why recovery from traumatic events has been so hard for you. CPT helps you learn how going through a trauma can change the way you look at the world, yourself, and others. The way we think and look at things directly affects how we feel and act. There are four things you need to do in order to be helped by CPT. First: educate yourself about your symptoms. Second: become more aware of your thoughts and feelings. Third: learn the skills necessary to help question or challenge your thoughts. Finally: learn about the common changes in beliefs that occur after going through trauma. This is more for people with Post Traumatic Stress Disorder, but God knows how far gone you are after a breakup. It is hard. If any of these terms resonate with you, research more. I simply don't want to bore the other readers with scientific jargon.

Prolonged Exposure Therapy takes a different approach to anxiety and stress. Instead of making you process the traumatic events cognitively, Prolonged Exposure Therapy makes you face your fears. By facing your fears, this form of therapy helps you break the connection between your negative memories and fear processing.

Prolonged Exposure Therapy requires you to gradually get closer and closer to the situation that led to the trauma. This therapy also uses computer graphics and virtual reality. This sounds like something I am going to have to try. Nevermind, I just looked up how much it is, and it's $150 a session. I'm not hurting too bad at the moment. Thank you.

These all sound great, but if you don't want to do this therapy, I suggest going for a bike ride. My therapy, if you can't tell, is writing. I write everything as a source of healing. Writing could be another form of therapy you could try. You can also get The Breakup Band Aid Workbook. It helps you journal. I think of everything.

You can even go to a support group like Alcoholics Anonymous since there isn't a real Exaholics Anonymous yet. They are very welcoming and amazing listeners.

You could even have a girl's night of pampering. Maybe even throw a passion party so you can get a spell-binding vibrator while you are on hiatus? Don't get one that does too many things or it will freak you out. I once got a vibrator where the head spun one way, beads on the shaft rotated the other way, and, of course, the vibrating elephant for your clit. Needless to say, I never use it because I have ADD and there is no way I can focus on all the gadgets turning inside of me all at once.

STEP BY STEP INSTRUCTIONS

1. Get a picture of your ex.
2. I know you still have one. Don't even lie, you cheater!
3. Buy a bag of ice.
4. Pour it into a tub of cold water.
5. Put your feet in the freezing ass water. Start to look at your ex's picture. This picture should remind you of what a cold-hearted prick they were to you. Feel how miserable you are when your feet are completely frozen. Keep them in the water for another three minutes until all you can think about when you see their picture is cold inscrutableness.
6. If it doesn't work, use the secret weapon of rotten eggs and mayonnaise. This one will work. I promise.
7. Get some rotten eggs.
8. Get mayonnaise.
9. Blend the two.
10. Maybe put some vinegar in there. Vinegar always smells like crap and makes me want to gag. Then, smell the concoction Now, rip up the photo and throw it away.

HELPFUL TIPS

1. Think of this as a science experiment. It will be fun!
2. Don't use new eggs. Make sure they are at least a few weeks expired.
3. If you don't eat eggs use something that smells raunchy and will make you gag, if not barf. Oh, rotten kale is a horrible one.

THE Breakup BAND AID

4. If you can, try to use a terrible picture of them. A hideous one where they are doing an obnoxious face or look like a nerd with a double chin.
5. Do this when no one is around because they might think you are crazy. You are, but you don't want people to believe that about you!

HOW Not TO USE THIS STEP

DO NOT EAT THE FOOD WHEN YOU ARE DONE! I mean you could possibly use the leftover ice to make margaritas. Make sure your feet were clean, or that would be disgusting.

I recommend not calling your ex to tell them what you are doing. It would not look cool on your part. This book is ALL about being cool. Let me tell you. You should be better by now anyway. Plus, if you called them that would be creepy, and they would probably hang up the phone on you. So, it's not worth it.

THIS STEP CURES ALL! No, it doesn't, but it's worth being optimistic. It should cure most though, because it is an excruciatingly disgusting step.

Again with this no story shit? What the hell kind of book is this?

STEP 12:
Wake Up and Smell the Coffee

WHAT THE HELL DOES THAT MEAN?

YOUR EX IS NEVER COMING BACK!!!!!! You know what is sad? Most of these breakup manuals are all directed towards women. Why do women have to be such emotional roller coasters? We are. We are hormonal and nervous breakdowns waiting to happen. And yes, I am aware this manual is geared toward women. I feel if men read it, they have done reckless crap too, and will be able to relate somewhat. Or have had to deal with crazy women that they still love.

    This step is about you. You and you alone need to think about what you want in life. If you want them, then you might as well go crawl in a hole and sulk in your own misery.

    Just have a damn realization already! You should be cured and help other heartbreakees who are in your shoes. Comfort them and be their sponsor. They might be ten times worse than you ever thought you were.

    I guess this step is all about helping others. I suggest adopting a dog. I want to do that, but my lovely roommate has two cats... so annoying.

THE Breakup BAND AID

STEP BY STEP INSTRUCTIONS

1. Read Chapter 1.
2. Read Chapter 2.
3. Read Chapter 3.
4. Read Chapter 4.
5. Read Chapter 5.
6. Read Chapter 6.
7. Read Chapter 7.
8. Read Chapter 8 and 9.
9. Read Chapter 10.
10. Read Chapter 11.

HELPFUL TIPS

1. Read this on your lunch break.
2. To absorb this book, you need to read it at least five times.
3. Take notes.
4. Sleep in.
5. Get off social media and go for a walk. Experience the beauty of life. Real life.

HOW Not TO USE THIS STEP

You can do whatever you want with your life. I am just saying it would be much easier to get over your ex and move on.

I never had an awakening, because I never had closure. The relationship was never off the table with us. We were always broken up, but still had love for each other. When you don't know why you broke up in the first place, it's much harder to get over the relationship. I think this is the first time I am being sentimental in this whole book. I have to be strong. I won't cry. The only good thing about our breakup is I fucked him up more than he did me. Not sure if that is true, I just like to think it is.

No matter what you do in this step, you can't go wrong. This was the step when I realized we weren't supposed to be together. I was always supposed to move to California and accomplish my dream.

If I would have stayed with him, God knows how miserable I would have been. We would have gotten married and probably had children. I would have gotten fat, and he would have cheated on me. We would likely get divorced, and I would be stuck with rugrats having no sex life.

I am not going to lie. I am over Eric. I mean I think it is comforting that he is around and still single. If he got married, then I guess I would try a little harder not to think about him. The good thing is I don't cry anymore. I don't stalk. I love knowing that there is another man out there ready to sweep me off my feet.

UPDATE: So over him, but am bound and determined to conquer the meat in LA. Look for my new book coming soon: Romances of an SAIF in LA. A SAIF is a Single, Attractive, Intelligent Female. Empowering women one dumb mistake at a time. It goes through my trials and tribulations of trying to date three men at once. If you thought my stories were crazy here, well just wait! Buckle up for a bumpy, crazy, funny, and absurd ride.

In summary, break up with everything that no longer suits your lifestyle. Break up with everyone who doesn't have your best interests at heart. Break up with habits that harm you and your mental health. Break up with the notion that there is no one out there for you than your ex. Break up with negativity. Break up with being sad. Smile, life throws us lessons to grow and learn from. The faster you learn these lessons, the less likely you will be to repeat them. You will finally have a true awakening. #Blessed

QUICK REFERENCE

Here is a quick reference guide if you are thinking about doing something irresponsible. If you are reading this, and are doing anything in the DON'T section, you better stop right now before you look like an idiot and get a restraining order against your crazy ass.

TWELVE STEP ONE-LINERS

1. Admit you are powerless over your ex.
2. Get rid of everything that reminds you of them.
3. Get a sponsor to help make sure you're not a trainwreck.
4. Make a list of what a spectacular catch you really are.
5. Admit what you did wrong in the relationship.
6. Don't contact or stalk your ex for sixty days.
7. Quit your bad habits.
8. Make a list of people to apologize to for being a trainwreck.
9. Then do it.
10. Don't fucking backslide! I mean it!
11. Sensory therapy. Your last-ditch effort.
12. Be refreshed, YOU DID IT! Your pain should be over.

DON'T EVER DO THESE THINGS, PSYCHO!

We are all crazy. I get it. It's hard not to be a psycho at moments. I am here to tell you it's not worth it. I wish it were. I do love being a Peyton McAdams, but people don't always care for that behavior.

I hope this is the most cohesive "Don't" list. I tried to think of everything possible you should never do to your ex after you break up. It is imperative that you never do these. They aren't smart. They are destructive. These are not meant to give you ideas. They are not good ideas you wish you thought of. They are horrible, scathing, sick, and demented thoughts drummed up by me. You are not allowed to use them.

WAYS OF CONTACT

1. Call them.
2. Call and hang up from a blocked number. Yes, they will know it's you.
3. Text them.
4. Facebook message them.
5. Tweet them.
6. Direct message them on Instagram.

THE Breakup BAND AID

7. Snapchat them.
8. Send them a childish lip-sync video on Musical.ly.
9. Join their Houseparty conversation.
10. Email them.
11. Hack into their email.
12. Write them a letter and mail it.
13. Stalk them.
14. Be where they will be.
15. I know you know where they will be, just don't go there, OK?
16. Fax them.
17. Send them a telegram.
18. Send them flowers.
19. Give them a shout out on the radio.
20. Put them on Ryan's Roses just so you can talk to them.
21. Make a fake profile on Facebook. Friend them and try to make them go on a date with you.
22. Write them a note and stick it under their door.
23. Get a plane to write a message across the sky.
24. Instant message them.
25. Skype them.
26. Call them over a loud speaker.
27. Call their work.
28. Go to their parent's house.
29. Contact them on LinkedIn.
30. Wiretap their house.
31. Add them to Find My Friends.
32. Install a Nanny Cam in their house.

GENERAL

1. Scream obscenities at them.
2. Google them.
3. Try to make them jealous with another suitor. It doesn't work unless the suitor is a super-hot neurosurgeon. In that case, you should be in heaven and no longer need this book.
4. Get them good seats at their favorite sporting event. They are going to take a friend with that extra ticket, not you!
5. Play tennis at their country club.

6. Be their caddy at a golf tournament.
7. Show up at their rugby tournament with cookies. (Maybe I did, maybe I didn't.)

EMOTIONAL STRESS

1. Write a mass blog about how they gave you herpes, even if it's true. I think there is a website where you can find out what celebrities have STDs.
2. Tell everyone you know he has a small penis and can only go for a minute and a half. If you are into women, tell everyone you know the girl is like screwing a dead fish.
3. Post sleazy get-back-at-them photos.
4. Find a really hot girl to hit on him, and when he thinks he is about to score with her, have her dump his ass. Same goes for dudes. You might actually make the girl cry, which would be a double bonus.
5. Delete all contacts in their phone.
6. Steal their ID so they can't go out.
7. Poke holes in their condom stash. Or maybe you can, because that is kind of hilarious. No, don't, I am a bad influence.
8. Put their profile on weird dating sites.
9. Put up an ad on Craigslist Missed Connections with their phone number.
10. Also post, Tweet, Instagram, and Snapchat their phone number to the world saying they are lonely and need a lot of sex.

BODILY HARM

1. Throw stuff at them.
2. Kick them.
3. Slap them across the face.
4. Throw a drink at them.
5. Gag them.
6. Try to poison them in any way.

THE Breakup BAND AID

7. Light them on fire.
8. Spit on them.
9. Send them Anthrax through the mail.
10. Replace their shampoo with hair remover.
11. Replace their mouthwash with Windex.
12. Put rubbing alcohol in their contact solution.
13. Hire a hit man to kill them.
14. Switch their pill bottles.

FRIENDS/FAMILY

1. Call up their mother and tell her what they did to you.
2. Call their friends and try to be buddies with them.
3. Date their sibling/parent.
4. Sleep with one of their friends.
5. Tell their spouse. Maybe you should do that, then they can dump them too and buy my book.
6. Pick their kids up from school.
7. Make out with their sibling's fiancé.
8. Throw their kids birthday parties, even if it is not their birthday.
9. Tell their friends that they always bad mouth them. Regurgitate word for word.
10. Tell their parents the nasty things you two used to do in bed, when your ex was supposed to be a virgin.

NEW GIRLFRIEND

1. Tell them how much better you are than their new girlfriend.
2. Call the new girlfriend and hang up.
3. Call the new girlfriend and call her a whore.
4. Call the new girlfriend and tell her that she has some STD.
5. Punch the new girlfriend at a bar.
6. Pull her hair. Pull out her hair extensions.
7. Snicker when she walks by you. Actually, that might be kind of funny. You have to do it every time she walks by. It will make her pissed. Again, don't do that. I am a bad influence.

8. Throw the new girlfriend over a banister.
9. Rip off her fake eyelashes.
10. Spread rumors about her, saying she is a hermaphrodite. Or any rumor for that matter.

NEW BOYFRIEND

1. Get in a fist fight. I feel that is probably all guys do to a new boyfriend.
2. Maybe they tell them that the chick has been calling them because their dick is bigger.
3. See new girlfriend, as well, just in case.

PETS

1. Put their cat in the microwave.
2. Boil their rabbit.
3. Kidnap their dog and hold for ransom.
4. Let their gerbil out into the wilderness.
5. Let the animals pee and poop all over their house.

HOUSE

1. Go to their house in the middle of the night, pound on their door, then dash.
2. Toilet paper their house.
3. Chalk up their driveway with obscenities and genitalia pics.
4. Steal their mailbox.
5. Put dog crap in their mailbox.
6. Camp out at their house and scare their neighbors.
7. Move into their apartment complex.
8. Make a banner saying "You Suck!" and hang it up on their front door. (Guilty. High School. Not me though. My girlfriends. In our defense, the dudes the next day thought it was guys from the opposing football team. #Winning)

THE Breakup BAND AID

9. Sneak into their apartment when they are not there and sleep in their bed.
10. Call the cops on them for a noise violation.
11. Spray grass killer on their lawn.
12. Paint their house with a different color paint.
13. Throw rocks at their window.
14. Throw eggs at it.
15. Throw garbage on their front lawn.
16. Pee in their pool.
17. Steal their video game collection.
18. Steal a road sign and put it in their yard.
19. Post a sign stating they were convicted of child molestation.
20. Poop in a bag and leave it outside their front door.
21. Have sex with someone in their bed and leave the used condom in the sheets.
22. Steal the cord from their Plasma TV.
23. Order porn on their Pay-Per-View. Lots and Lots of porn.
24. Call Japan from their landline and leave.
25. Dump out all of their plants on the floor.
26. Spill red wine on the carpet.
27. Put a picture of you up on top of the mantel piece.
28. Unplug their refrigerator.
29. Turn on all the outdoor spigots and leave.
30. Cut down a tree and let it fall on the house.
31. Put algae in their pool.

CAR

1. Slash their tires.
2. Let air out of their tires. That is more conspicuous.
3. Put a nail in their tire. Everyone drives over nails.
4. Shaving cream their car. It takes off the paint. (Or so I have heard.)
5. Put water in their gas tank.
6. Key your name on their driver's side door.
7. Tow their car.
8. Put a boot on their tire.
9. Put Vaseline on their steering wheel.

10. Beat the shit out of their car with a bat.
11. Throw rocks at their windshield.
12. Smash the headlights.
13. Steal the driver's side mirror.

CLOTHES

1. Bleach all their laundry.
2. Rip buttons off all of their shirts.
3. Tie knots in their shoelaces.
4. Cut their ties.
5. Rip their pant zippers.
6. Cut holes in all their underwear.
7. Torch the clothes in a bonfire.
8. Throw paint on their clothes.

WORK/GYM/HANGOUT/EVENTS

1. Show up at their place of work, looking totally hot.
2. Call their work and tell their boss that they have been stealing company time.
3. Call their work and tell them that your ex quit.
4. Get a job where they work.
5. Go to their graduation party uninvited.
6. Sign up at their gym.
7. Get a job at the coffee place they go to before work.
8. Go to their family reunion, or any family gatherings for that matter. Including funerals.
9. Break all the machines at the gym so they can't use them.
10. Go to their wedding.

MONEY

1. Steal their mail so they are late on their bills.
2. Max out their credit cards.

THE Breakup BAND AID

3. Send bank account info over social media. If you don't know their bank account number, send their social security number.
4. Order a shit ton of stuff on their Amazon account.
5. Loan them money.

YOU

1. Buy a shirt, spray their cologne on it and sniff it every night before you go to bed.
2. Fake a pregnancy to get him back (Obviously this only works for females, trying to be gender neutral does not always work. Sorry men.)
3. Fake a death in the family to get them to comfort you.
4. Photoshop yourself into pictures your ex just posted on Facebook.
5. Binge eat.
6. Internet date. Those assholes just want sex.
7. Make a collage of photos of you and your ex; a shrine to show your love for one another.
8. Start an Instagram war with them. An Instagram war is when they post a picture and you duplicate it, but try to make it better. Let's say the post a picture of them next to a nice brick wall, you then post a picture of you by a brick wall with a mural. Celeste Barber has mastered this.

SLUTTY

1. Make out with a guy in front of him. It may seem like a good idea at the time, but it's tacky and tasteless. Same goes for dudes.
2. Send them nude photos of yourself.
3. Send them dick pics, no one really likes a dick pic, especially when we all know they are recycled.

DO THESE INSTEAD

Once again, I tried to put together the most cohesive list I could think of to get your mind off this lame insignificant breakup. The most important thing is to keep yourself busy with activities you love to do. Try new things during this period. You will learn what you want out of life and what you don't.

ACTIVITIES/ATTRACTIONS

1. Help out at a homeless shelter.
2. Help out at an animal shelter.
3. Visit museums.
4. Visit haunted places.
5. Get it all out at the batting cages.
6. Play miniature golf.
7. Go bowling.
8. Bring toys to the children's hospital.
9. Go whale watching.
10. Go to amusement parks.
11. Travel to foreign lands.
12. Take a road trip.
13. Go wine tasting.

THE *Breakup* BAND AID

14. Try laser tag.
15. Play paintball.
16. Visit a farmer's market.
17. Join a volleyball league.
18. Join a softball league.
19. Go to a pro sporting event.
20. Go to a concert.
21. Rock Climb.
22. Skydive (or simulation).
23. Ride the mechanical bull at whatever bar has one.
24. Go sailing.
25. Go parasailing.
26. Go ziplining.
27. Go horseback riding.
28. Get tickets to Cirque Du Soleil.
29. See a comedy show.
30. See an improv show.
31. Have a girls' night out with cocktails at a posh lounge.
32. Deliver Meals on Wheels.
33. Then there is always Las Vegas.
34. Watch an orchestra.
35. Watch an opera.
36. Go to Burning Man.
37. Attend the Olympics.
38. Learn how to scuba dive.
39. Fly in a hot air balloon.
40. Jump in a pool fully clothed.
41. Do a charity walk.
42. Plant a tree.
43. Go wine tasting.

FUN HOBBIES/CLASSES

1. Painting.
2. Pottery.
3. Cooking.
4. Book Club.
5. Join a choir.

6. Join a play.
7. Photography.
8. Learn a foreign language.
9. Self-defense.
10. Writing.
11. Learn how to sew.
12. Learn how to knit or crochet.
13. Salsa lessons.
14. Computer training.
15. Graphic design.
16. Surf lessons.
17. Shop class.
18. Auto mechanics. Good to have when jerkoffs try to rip you off.
19. Psych class.
20. Sociology class.
21. Critical analysis of popular diets class.
22. Learn how to sail.

EX

1. Get rid of "their" friends.
2. Unfriend on Facebook. Unfollow on any social media.
3. Block them on all social media.
4. Delete their number/email/etc. Just do it for right now, because I know you are going to put it back in later.
5. Get a new phone number. It will help you not call them, because you don't want them to have your new number. It also helps you to stalk. No, I am kidding, you better not do that!
6. Burn all of their shit right away.

PAMPERING

1. Teeth whitening.
2. Tanning/Spray tanning. I am addicted to spray tanning. It helps me look less transparent and veiny.

3. Infrared sauna.
4. Red light therapy.
5. Massage.
6. Microdermabrasion.
7. Photofacial.
8. Regular facial.
9. Laser facial.
10. Pretty much any laser thing you can think of that they have now.
11. Cut/color hair.
12. Mani/pedi.
13. Full body waxing.
14. Foot massage.
15. Seaweed wrap.
16. Mud bath.
17. Body scrub.
18. Laser hair removal.
19. Invisalign (if needed).
20. Get a new outfit.
21. Get a new perfume.
22. Endermologie.

HEALTH/FITNESS

1. Get a colonic.
2. Eat five servings of fruits and vegetables a day.
3. Drink more water. It will flush out your toxins.
4. Yoga.
5. Bikram yoga.
6. Pilates.
7. No gravity Pilates.
8. Go for a hike.
9. Pole Dancing.
10. Cardio Barre/Bar Method.
11. Spinning.
12. Zumba.
13. Cardio kickboxing.
14. Belly dancing.

15. Hip hop dance.
16. Burlesque class.
17. Aerobics.
18. Orange Theory.
19. Circuit training.
20. CrossFit.
21. Go to a track and do interval training.
22. Run a 5k.
23. Bike ride.
24. Rollerblade. Do people still do that?
25. Snowboard/Ski.
26. Swimming.
27. Surfing.
28. Weight training.
29. Lose weight (if needed).

IT'S A STAY·AT·HOME KIND OF NIGHT

1. Clean out the clutter.
2. Organize.
3. Light a candle and take a bubble bath while listening to some beautiful classical music.
4. Do crossword puzzles. (I prefer People Magazine. It's easy.)
5. Watch trashy reality TV. Real Housewives comes to mind. It will make you feel so much better about yourself.
6. Read a good mystery. James Patterson is amazing in this area.
7. Experiment with a vibrator.
8. Watch SATC season 1 & 2 and pretend you are Samantha.
9. Put on a face mask.
10. Drink a glass of wine.

WORK/SCHOOL

1. Get overtime if you can. You are gonna need some extra cash.
2. Take a fun class. See FUN HOBBIES/CLASSES.
3. Study and get on the Dean's List.

THE *Breakup* BAND AID

4. Challenge yourself.
5. Take on an extra task.
6. Send someone you hate a nice email.
7. Bring in cookies to share.
8. Work on getting a promotion.

MISCELLANOUS

1. Move.
2. Learn the rules of football.
3. Go to a red-light party.
4. Throw a red-light party.
5. Try online dating. Do not get frustrated. Know that some of them are going to be doozies.
6. Go on a blind date with no expectations. (See #5.)

TRAVEL BUCKET LIST

In my opinion, since I started traveling a little over a year ago, this is literally the best thing you can do for yourself and your mental health. Research. Look up amazing blogs. You can find anything on the internet, even if you are on a budget. I don't want to waste my time sulking over a man. I want to travel and experience life.

This section is a quick travel bucket list to inspire you. My bucket list includes all travel, especially obscure places. I have things I want to achieve in my life, and one is to publish a book. Your bucket list can be anything and everything you want. There is no right or wrong. Have fun. You will be excited to see how much you accomplish on your bucket list once you make one. I even put movies I want to watch and books I want to read. I feel accomplished every time I put a check mark next to an activity.

Get all your girlfriends together, drink wine and research bucket lists. Whatever your little heart desires, put it in. Let's get going; we have shit to do, and people to see. My one girlfriend's goal is to sleep with a man on every continent. She has accomplished three! Boom. Let's do this! Let's do this.

THE *Breakup* BAND AID

NORTH AMERICA

- ❑ Ride a cable car in San Francisco
- ❑ Drive up the PCH in California in a convertible
- ❑ Road trip around the USA
- ❑ Lake Tahoe, California
- ❑ Joshua Tree, California
- ❑ Drive Route 66, USA
- ❑ Disneyland, California
- ❑ Summer in the Hamptons, New York
- ❑ New Year's in Times Square, New York
- ❑ Ice skate at Rockefeller Plaza, New York
- ❑ Central Park, New York
- ❑ Niagara Falls, New York
- ❑ Las Vegas, Nevada
- ❑ Yellowstone National Park, Wyoming
- ❑ Camp in Wyoming
- ❑ Mount Rushmore, South Dakota
- ❑ Haiku Stairs of Oahu, Hawaii
- ❑ Mardi Gras in New Orleans, Louisiana
- ❑ Washington, DC
- ❑ Dogsled in Alaska
- ❑ Wear a ridiculous hat to the Kentucky Derby, Kentucky (Obviously.)
- ❑ Hike Appalachian trail in Maine.
- ❑ Nashville, Tennessee
- ❑ Pig Island, Bahamas
- ❑ The Great Blue Hole, Belize
- ❑ Spring Break in Cabo San Lucas, Mexico
- ❑ Sayulita, Mexico
- ❑ Zipline in Costa Rica

SOUTH AMERICA

- ❑ Machu Picchu, Peru
- ❑ Go to the Carnival in Rio De Janeiro, Brazil
- ❑ Stand on the Equator, Brazil

- ☐ Amazon Rainforest, Brazil
- ☐ Galapagos Islands, Ecuador
- ☐ Easter Island, Chile
- ☐ Montevideo, Uruguay

AFRICA

- ☐ Four Seasons Safari Lodge, Serengeti, Tanzania
- ☐ Great Pyramids of Giza, Egypt
- ☐ The Lighthouse of Alexandria, Egypt
- ☐ Shower in Victoria Falls, Zambia
- ☐ Go on a Safari (Google where to go, I am sure there is a ton all over.)
- ☐ Giraffe Manor, Kenya

EUROPE

- ☐ Ride a gondola in Italy
- ☐ Stomp grapes on a vineyard in Tuscany, Italy
- ☐ Sistine Chapel, Vatican City, Italy
- ☐ Oktoberfest in Germany
- ☐ Smoke weed in Amsterdam, then go to the Van Gogh Museum. (Trust me!)
- ☐ Greece. Anywhere and Everywhere.
- ☐ Ireland
- ☐ Kayak the Blue Lagoon in Turkey.
- ☐ Stay in an over water bungalow in Bora Bora
- ☐ Eiffel Tower in Paris, France
- ☐ London, England
- ☐ Stonehenge, England
- ☐ Tunnel of love in Klevan, Ukraine
- ☐ Sleep in a Castle in Scotland
- ☐ See the northern lights in Norway
- ☐ Saint Petersburg, Russia
- ☐ Switzerland. Anywhere and Everywhere.
- ☐ Iceland

THE *Breakup* BAND AID

ASIA

- ☐ Great Wall of China
- ☐ Let go of a floating lantern in China
- ☐ Swim in the Dead Sea
- ☐ Taj Mahal in India
- ☐ Ride a camel in Abu Dhabi
- ☐ Climb Mount Everest, Nepal
- ☐ Angkor Wat, Cambodia
- ☐ The Hang Son Doong Cave in Vietnam
- ☐ Sea of Stars in Vaadhoo Island in Maldives
- ☐ Songkran Festival in Thailand

AUSTRALIA

- ☐ Great Barrier Reef
- ☐ Queensland
- ☐ Sydney

TOP 10 LIST

BREAKUPS THROUGHOUT HISTORY

This section is important because I want to show you that everyone goes through breakups and survives them. It might feel like a kick in the keister at the moment or a jab in the heart, whatever analogy you want to make during this difficult time. If you want, make a list of all the breakups you can think of on your own. It might be helpful. Plus, I wrote this list like five years ago and didn't feel like updating it. As you will see in parentheses, some of them decided they needed to get back together.

CELEBRITIES

1. Brad Pitt and the two huge A-listers
2. Sonny and Cher
3. Nicole Kidman and Tom Cruise
4. Kim Basinger and Alec Baldwin
5. Christie Brinkley and Billy Joel
6. Elizabeth Taylor and her eight men
7. Jennifer Lopez and a lot of men
8. Susan Sarandon and Tim Robbins
9. Demi Moore and Bruce Willis
10. Sandra Bullock and that douche bag

REALITY STARS

1. Simon Cowell and American Idol
2. Caitlyn Jenner and Keeping Up with the Kardashians
3. All the Bachelors (Except what? Two?)
4. All the Bachelorettes (Except what? Two?)
5. Hugh Hefner and his 97 girlfriends (May he rest in peace)
6. John and Kate Gosselin
7. I feel like a lot of Real Housewives always divorce too.
8. Hulk Hogan and his wife Linda
9. Carmen Electra and Dave Navarro
10. Heidi Montag and Spencer Pratt (Did they get back together?)

TWEEN IDOL STARS

1. Justin Timberlake and Britney Spears
2. Zac Efron and Vanessa Hudgens
3. Jessica Simpson and Nick Lachey
4. Nick Carter and Paris Hilton
5. Demi Lovato and Joe Jonas
6. Selena Gomez and Justin Bieber (Twice.)
7. Taylor Swift and Jake Gyllenhaal
8. Penn Bagley and Blake Lively
9. Miley Cyrus and Liam Hemsworth (Again, with these fuckers getting back together and screwing up my list.)
10. Scarlett Johansson and Ryan Reynolds

ATHLETES

1. Tiger Woods and Elin Nordegren
2. Andy Roddick and Mandy Moore
3. LeBron James and the Cleveland Cavaliers (Twice.)
4. Joe DiMaggio and Marilyn Monroe
5. Common and Serena Williams
6. Tony Parker and Eva Longoria
7. Chris Webber and Tyra Banks

THE Breakup BAND AID

8. Lance Armstrong and Sheryl Crow
9. Derek Jeter and Mariah Carey
10. Kobe Bryant and Brandy

POLITICIANS

1. Maria Shriver and Arnold Schwarzenegger
2. Hillary Clinton and the GOP
3. John and Elizabeth Edwards
4. Eliot Spitzer and Silda Wall
5. Mark and Jenny Sanford
6. Rudy Giuliani and Donna Hanover
7. Donald Trump and Ivana (Since he's a politician now.)
8. Al and Tipper Gore
9. Newt Gingrich and Marianne Ginther
10. John and Carol McCain

BANDS

1. Destiny's Child
2. *NSync
3. The Beatles
4. Simon and Garfunkel
5. The Supremes
6. Led Zeppelin
7. The Police
8. Journey
9. Blondie
10. Lonestar

BREAKUP SONGS

Some people do retail therapy to heal a broken heart. I prefer music. When I am in the depression stage, I listen to the saddest songs on the planet so I can cry out all of my tears. Does that help you lose weight? Does it make your metabolism soar? I should find out for you. Then I go through the "Fuck you, I am better than you," phase. Where I jam out and get my body back in shape. There are so many amazing songs that will empower you. Here are just a few. As stated previously, these might be dated, so you can make a new list if you want. Obviously, though, some of them are natural classics that will never go out of style.

FOR HIM

1. Bob Marley and The Wailers – "No Woman, No Cry"
2. Puddle of Mudd – "She Hates Me"
3. Foo Fighters – "The One"
4. Jay-Z – "99 Problems"
5. Marvin Gaye – "I Heard It Through the Grapevine"
6. Muse – "Feeling Good"
7. Simple Plan – "When I'm Gone"
8. Three Days Grace – "(I Hate) Everything About You"

THE Breakup BAND AID

9. Theory of a Deadman – "Me and My Girl"
10. Guns N' Roses – "Back Off Bitch"
    Bonus: Chris Cornell – "Part of Me"

ANGRY

1. Papa Roach – "Burn"
2. Brand New – "Seventy Times 7"
3. My Chemical Romance – "I'm Not Okay (I Promise)"
4. Nickelback – "Never Again"
5. Maroon 5 – "Wake Up Call"
6. The All-American Rejects – "Gives You Hell"
7. Limp Bizkit – "Break Stuff"
8. No Doubt – "Ex-Girlfriend"
9. Bon Jovi – "You Give Love a Bad Name"
10. EMF – "Unbelievable"

ROCK

1. Journey – "Separate Ways (Worlds Apart)"
2. Whitesnake – "Here I Go Again"
3. Led Zeppelin – "Babe I'm Gonna Leave You"
4. Poison – "Every Rose Has its Thorns"
5. Metallica – "Nothing Else Matters"
6. Rolling Stones – "Under My Skin"
7. Bad Company – "Gone, Gone, Gone"
8. R.E.M. – "The One I Love"
9. Def Leppard – "Love Bites"
10. The Police – "Every Breath You Take"

EMPOWERING BREAKUP SONGS (To workout to and get pissed!)

1. Carrie Underwood – "Before He Cheats"
2. Destiny's Child – "Survivor"

3. Gloria Gaynor – "I Will Survive"
4. Christina Aguilera – "Fighter"
5. Pat Benatar – "Heartbreaker"
6. Pink – "U + Ur Hand"
7. Black Eyed Peas – "Shut Up"
8. Britney Spears – "She'll Never Be Me"
9. Britney Spears – "Stronger"
10. Alanis Morissette – "You Oughta Know" (pretty popular blog song apparently)

EMPOWERING BREAKUP SONGS PART 2 (Because this deserves another round.)

1. Kelly Clarkson – "Since U Been Gone"
2. Jody Watley – "Looking for a New Love"
3. Kim Wilde – "Keep Me Hanging On"
4. Kelly Clarkson – "Never Again"
5. Justin Timberlake – "Cry Me a River"
6. Cee-Lo Green – "Fuck You"
7. Janis Joplin – "Piece of My Heart"
8. Reba McIntyre – "Take It Back"
9. Patty Loveless – "Blame It on Your Heart"
10. Miranda Lambert – "Gunpowder & Lead"

EMPOWERING BREAKUP SONGS PART 3 (And one more for reinforcement.)

1. Lady Gaga – "Bad Romance"
2. Michelle Branch – "Are You Happy Now"
3. Rihanna – "Breaking Dishes"
4. Blu Cantrell – "Hit 'Em Up Style"
5. LaToya – "She Ain't Got Shit"
6. Aly & AJ – "Potential Breakup Song"
7. Jazmin Sullivan – "Bust Your Windows"
8. Joss Stone – "You Had Me"
9. Beyoncé – "Irreplaceable"
10. Alicia Keys – "Karma"

THE Breakup BAND AID

SADDEST

1. PM Dawn – "Die Without You"
2. Dru Hill – "I love you"
3. Harry Nilsson – "Without You"
4. Coldplay – "The Scientist"
5. Coldplay – "Trouble"
6. Eric Carmen – "All by Myself"
7. No Doubt – "Don't Speak"
8. Sheryl Crow – "The First Cut is the Deepest"
9. Fleetwood Mac – "Silver Springs"
10. Adele – "Rolling in the Deep" (pretty much her first two albums)

SADDEST PART 2 (Cause you're probably gonna wallow for a while.)

1. Shirley Bassey – "I"
2. Elton John – "Sorry Seems to Be the Hardest Word"
3. Boyz II Men – "On Bended Knee"
4. *NSync –" Gone"
5. Bonnie Raitt – "I Can't Make You Love Me"
6. Adele – "Someone Like You"
7. Journey – "Open Arms"
8. 3 Doors Down – "Here Without You"
9. Hinder – "Better Than Me"
10. Air Supply – "All Out of Love"

SADDEST PART 3 (We all need a good cry sometimes.)

1. Bon Jovi – "This Ain't a Love Song"
2. Amy Winehouse – "Back to Black"
3. Gary Allen – "Best I Ever Had"
4. Avril Lavigne – "Fall to Pieces"
5. Roxette – "It Must've Been Love"
6. Chicago – "Look Away"

7. Nazareth – "Love Hurts"
8. John Waite – "Missing You"
9. Wynonna Judd – "Is It Over Yet"
10. Backstreet Boys – "Incomplete"

COUNTRY

1. Keith Urban – "You'll Think of Me"
2. The Wreckers – "Leave the Pieces"
3. Taylor Swift – "Teardrops on My Guitar" (And every other Taylor Swift song ever written. Also, when Swifty was country.)
4. Rascal Flatts – "What Hurts the Most"
5. Brad Paisley – "Whiskey Lullaby"
6. Miranda Lambert – "Your Mama's Broken Heart"
7. Willie Nelson – "Always on My Mind"
8. Patsy Cline – "Crazy"
9. Garth Brooks – "The Dance"
10. Tim McGraw – "Please Remember Me"

BEST LOVE SONGS (Only listen to in the depression stage.)

1. Jeff Healy Band – "Angel Eyes"
2. Coldplay – "Yellow"
3. Coldplay – "Sparks"
4. Eric Clapton – "You Look Wonderful Tonight"
5. Whitney Houston – "I Will Always Love You"
6. Jimmy Eat World – "For Me This is Heaven"
7. 3 Doors Down – "When I'm Gone"
8. Aerosmith – "Angel"
9. Richard Marx – "Right Here Waiting for You"
10. John Michael Montgomery – "I Love the Way You Love Me"

THE Breakup BAND AID

OTHERS TO CONSIDER

1. 4 Seasons – "Big Girls Don't Cry"
2. Eminem – "Love the Way You Lie feat. Rihanna"
3. Lady Antebellum – "Need You Now"
4. Usher – "Burn"
5. Carly Simon – "You're So Vain"
6. Jewel – "Foolish Games"
7. Toni Braxton – "Un-Break My Heart"
8. Miley Cyrus – "FU"
9. Big Sean – "I Don't Fuck with You"
10. Sam Smith – "I'm Not the Only One"

BREAKUP BOOKS

I did not put self-help books on this list. I feel you probably bought those already. These are books I enjoyed reading. Some might be completely unrelated to breakups. They may be able to help you crack a smile, cry hysterically, or give you a lesson in literature.

FICTION

1. Jane Austen – *Emma*
2. Elena Ferrante – *The Days of Abandonment*
3. David Levithan – *The Lover's Dictionary*
4. Julie Buxbaum – *The Opposite of Love*
5. Liane Moriarty – *What Alice Forgot*
6. Deb Caletti – *He's Gone*
7. Nancy Mitford – *Love in a Cold Climate*
8. Sharon Phennah – *You Can't Iron a Wrinkled Birthday Suit*
9. Lionel Shriver – *The Post-Birthday World*
10. Lorrie Moore – *Self-Help*

NON·FICTION

1. Christine Stevens – *Love*
2. Annais Nin – *The Diary of Annais Nin*
3. Elizabeth Gilbert – *Eat, Pray Love: One Woman's Search for Everything Across Italy, India, and Indonesia*
4. Chelsea Handler – *My Horizontal Life: A Collection of One-Night Stands*
5. Julie Klausner – *I Don't Care About Your Band*
6. Robert Greene – *The Art of Seduction*
7. Jenny Lawson – *Let's Pretend This Never Happened*
8. Mindy Kaling – *Is Everyone Hanging Out Without Me? (And Other Concerns)*
9. David Sedaris – *Me Talk Pretty One Day*
10. Jen Lancaster – *Such a Pretty Fat*

BREAKUP MOVIES

A lot of these movies are not breakup movies. Your breakup could play out like a romantic comedy. Think of this breakup as the first 15 pages of a script. Your breakup was your inciting incident. You can go through the script trying to get your ex back and failing miserably until the last shot where the person of your dreams comes in and carries you away on horse at sunset.

REVENGE

1. 'The War of the Roses'
2. 'Fatal Attraction'
3. 'Thelma and Louise'
4. 'American Psycho'
5. 'Closer'
6. 'The Break-Up'
7. 'Carrie'
8. 'Misery'
9. 'Strangers on a Train'
10. 'Basic Instinct'

DEPRESSING

1. 'Eternal Sunshine of the Spotless Mind'
2. 'Hope Floats'
3. '(500) Days of Summer'
4. 'Casablanca'
5. 'The End of the Affair'
6. 'Kramer Vs. Kramer'
7. 'The Apartment'
8. 'The Way We Were'
9. 'Ghost'
10. 'Romeo and Juliet'
11. 'Titanic'

EMPOWERING/COMEDIC

1. 'Bridget Jones's Diary'
2. 'Sliding Doors'
3. 'The Holiday'
4. 'The Breakup Band Aid (Coming Soon! Well, maybe, in like a year or two.)'
5. 'How to Lose a Guy in Ten Days'
6. 'He's Just Not That into You'
7. 'The Wedding Singer'
8. 'Bridesmaids'
9. 'Sweet Home Alabama'
10. 'When Harry Met Sally'
11. 'Pretty Woman'

MUSICAL

1. 'Gold Diggers of 1933'
2. 'On the Town'
3. 'Singin' in the Rain'
4. 'High Society'
5. 'My Fair Lady'

6. 'Funny Girl'
7. 'Hello, Dolly!'
8. 'Grease'
9. 'Dirty Dancing'
10. 'A Star is Born' – Probably all of them since there's like four.

GUY

1. 'Swingers'
2. 'High Fidelity'
3. 'Better off Dead'
4. 'Good Will Hunting'
5. 'Mallrats'
6. 'Chasing Amy'
7. 'Heat'
8. 'Blood Simple'
9. 'Forgetting Sarah Marshall'
10. 'The 40-Year-Old Virgin'

ROMANCE

1. 'Some Like It Hot'
2. 'It Happened One Night'
3. 'Camille'
4. 'The Shop Around the Corner'
5. 'The Philadelphia Story'
6. 'Random Harvest'
7. 'An Affair to Remember'
8. 'Pillow Talk'
9. 'While You Were Sleeping'
10. 'An Officer and a Gentlemen'

FAMOUS BREAKUP QUOTES

When I told you this book has everything I could possibly think of to help get you over a breakup, I meant it. These are the best quotes I found on the internet. If there is one I am missing, feel free to email thebreakupbandaid@gmail.com. I don't want you to get overwhelmed with these, so read just a few at a time and go back. There are a lot and could get tiring or cumbersome. I don't ever want you to get bored, so if you are, skip this. I know there has been a lot of information these past few hours. This is still part of the top 10 lists. I just gave you a few extra! As always, you're welcome.

CELEBRITIES

"I love to shop after a bad relationship. I buy a new outfit and it makes me feel better. Sometimes I see a really great outfit, I'll break up with someone on purpose."

- Rita Rudner

"Nothing takes the taste out of peanut butter quite like unrequited love."

- Charlie Brown

"Pleasure of love lasts but a moment, pain of love lasts a lifetime."

- Bette Davis

"If you're a woman living, you've been done wrong by a man."
- Oprah Winfrey

"Only time can heal your broken heart as only time can heal his broken arms and legs."
- Miss Piggy

"I've had heartaches, headaches, toothaches, earaches, and I've had a few pains in the ass; but I've survived to tell about it."
- Dolly Parton

"To fall in love is awfully simple, but to fall out of love is simply awful."
- Bess Myerson

"Time wounds all heels."
- Jane Ace

"I don't need anyone to rectify my existence. The most profound relationship we will ever have is the one with ourselves."
- Shirley MacLaine

"It's better to be unhappy alone than unhappy with someone - so far."
- Marilyn Monroe

"Save a boyfriend for a rainy day. And another, in case it doesn't rain."
- Mae West

MOVIES/TV SHOWS

"There is a good way to breakup with someone and it doesn't include a post-it."
- Sex and the City

"Hearts will never be practical until they are made unbreakable."
- Wizard of Oz

"Frankly, my dear, I don't give a damn."
- Gone with The Wind

THE Breakup BAND AID

"A relationship, I think, is like a shark. You know? It has to constantly move forward or it dies. And I think what we got on our hands is a dead shark."

- Annie Hall

BANDS/SINGERS/SONGWRITERS

"As soon as forever is through, I'll be over you."

- Toto

"Every rose has its thorn."

- Bret Michaels

"You think I'd crumble. You think I'd lay down and die. Oh no, not I, I will survive."

- Gloria Gaynor

"Love is like a brick, you can build a house or sink a dead body."

- Lady Gaga

"You had a good girl, good girl but didn't know how to treat her. So silly boy get out my face. Why do you like the way regret taste?"

- Rihanna

"From an angel's wings to a fallen star, God makes everything but unbreakable hearts."

- Jessica Andrews

"I never knew how quickly I would go from someone that you loved to someone you used to know."

- Collin Raye

WRITERS/POETS

"The heart was made to be broken."

- Oscar Wilde

SARAH MELLAND

"For all sad words of tongue and pen, the saddest are these, 'It might have been'."

- John Greenleaf Whittier

"Never regret. If it's good, it's wonderful. If it's bad, it's experience."

- Victoria Holt

"To survive it is often necessary to fight and to fight you have to dirty yourself."

- George Orwell

DEPRESSION

"God is closest to those with broken hearts."

- Jewish expression

"Love begins with a smile, grows with a kiss, and ends with a teardrop."

- St. Augustin

"Heavy hearts, like heavy clouds in the sky, are best relieved by the letting of a little water."

- Antoine Rivarol

"Yes, I will go. I would rather grieve over your absence than over you."

- Antonio Porchia

"It amazes me so that we enter a relationship whole and leave it only a half."

- Tigress Luv

DENIAL

"Ever has it been that love knows not its own depth until the hour of separation."

- Kahlil Gibran

"Sad endings are but the next happy beginning."

- Jhan

"Never be sad for what is over, just be glad that it was once yours."
- Anonymous

"Missing you isn't the hard part, knowing I once had you is what breaks my heart."
- Anonymous

"I would like to stay a secret, like walking in the dark, if no one knows you, no one cares and no one breaks your heart."
- Anonymous

"If you're going to make me cry, at least be there to wipe away the tears."
- Anonymous

ANGER

"Pain is inevitable. Suffering is optional."
- Haruki Murakami

"If you can't save the relationship, at least save your pride."
- Anonymous

"The hottest love has the coldest end."
- Socrates

"An eye for an eye leaves the whole world blind."
- Gandhi

*Fun fact: This actually might not be a Gandhi quote, but by his biographer Larry Fischer. He used this quote as an explanation of Gandhi's philosophy.

"He who angers you conquers you."
- Elizabeth Kenny

BARGAINING

"Relationships are like glass. Sometimes it's better to leave them broken than try to hurt yourself putting it back together."

- Anonymous

"The greatest experiences of your life are not usually welcome ones."

- Anonymous

"When you are in love and you get hurt, it's like a cut… it will heal, but there will always be a scar."

- Anonymous

"When you are sorrowful look again in your heart, and you shall see that in truth you are weeping for that which has been your delight."

- Kahlil Gibran

"In the arithmetic of love, one plus one equals everything, and two minus one equals nothing."

- Mignon McLaughlin

"Bargaining has neither friends nor relations."

- Benjamin Franklin

INSPIRATIONAL/HEALING

"Every happy couple has a breakup in their past."

- Anonymous

"If someone you love hurts you, cry a river, build a bridge, and get over it."

- Anonymous

"My mind tells me to give up on love, but my heart won't let me."

- Anonymous

"To love and win is the best thing. To love and lose, the next best."

- William M. Thackeray

FUNNY

"The minute you settle for less than you deserve, you get even less than you settled for."
- Maureen Dowd

"The good thing about breaking up is that you have nothing else to lose."
- Sammy Hagar

"I ran into my ex the other day, put it in reverse, and hit him again!"
- Anonymous

"Guys are like Slinkies: good for nothing but it's funny when they fall down the stairs."
- Anonymous

"If payback is a bitch and revenge is sweet then I'm the sweetest bitch you will ever meet."
- Anonymous

"Smile. Tomorrow will be worse."
- Murphy's Law

"My 'Once Upon a Time' didn't end 'Happily Ever After.'"
- Anonymous

AMAZING COMFORT FOOD

Right after the breakup, most of you will barely be able to breathe let alone eat. There are a select few breakees who like to drown their sorrows in food. I am here to say, stop!

I will let you take a week and do as much damage as you need. After a week, I will walk you through an easy meal plan to burn off the ten pounds you gained. Another random fact I would like to throw in, your body will lose those excess pounds pretty quickly. Your body wants to stay at a constant. If you gained the weight quickly, you will be able to drop it quicker. If you have been carrying extra poundage for a few years now, it's going to be a little more of an uphill battle, but we will conquer it together.

Disastrous Calorie Counters – These foods are my absolute favorite. I only eat them on my cheat days, which are somewhat frequently depending on my mood.

INDULGENT FOODS

- Spinach dip from Trader Joe's (The frozen one in a green box.)
- Thin crust pepperoni pizza by DiGiorno
- Quepapas from Pizza Hut
- Garlic herb chicken wings also from Pizza Hut

- Fried macaroni balls from The Cheesecake Factory
- Oreo pie from Edwards (In your grocer's freezer.)
- Moose tracks ice cream
- Cheesy fiesta potatoes from Taco Bell
- Tuna melts from any great café with French fries and ranch dressing

EASY MEAL PLAN

In order to lose weight, you also need to exercise. I have given you my personal favorites in previous chapters. I also recommend a calorie counter. There are apps on your phone to do it for you.

If you are willing to never cheat on your diet, you don't need a calorie counter. If you never eat processed foods, you should be good. I mean basically sticking to vegetables, quinoa, salmon, and nuts. Fruits have too much sugar, so I would only eat them in the morning.

BREAKFAST CHOICES

- Egg whites
- Avocado toast on sprouted bread
- Oatmeal
- Fresh fruit
- High fiber cereal
- Green smoothies
- Turkey sausage

LUNCH CHOICES

- Turkey hummus wrap
- Black bean soup
- Salmon salad with arugula
- Veggie burger with sweet potato fries
- Veggie pita

- Grilled chicken wrap
- Shrimp skewers
- Steamed Veggies
- Whole wheat turkey sandwich
- Chili
- Salads with lemon and olive oil dressing. No processed or creamy dressing.

SNACK CHOICES

- Small meal replacement bar
- Low-fat coconut yogurt
- Sugar free Jell-O w/tbsp. of whipped cream
- Sorbet
- Rice cake
- ½ cup of soaked almonds
- Small granola bar
- 1 tbsp. of almond butter with celery
- 100 calorie popcorn
- A handful of carrots with hummus
- Chia pudding
- Oven-roasted garbanzo beans

DINNER CHOICES

- Chicken fajitas
- Grilled chicken and steamed broccoli
- Turkey meatballs with oven-roasted Brussels sprouts
- Grilled salmon with asparagus
- Minestrone soup
- Coconut quinoa curry
- Zucchini noodles with pesto

THE Breakup BAND AID

Google for more healthy choice recipe options. I try to stay on an alkaline diet for numerous reasons. My eyes are pure white. I have so much more energy and look more vibrant. My favorite alkaline diet cookbooks are by Live Energized. Plus, I drink water like there is no tomorrow. Proper hydration will help you lose those excess pounds.

Always research and find what program will work best for you. These options have worked for me, and I have lost 50 pounds at my heaviest. It did not happen all in the same year. They were pretty spaced out. So, don't ever worry about that. Stick to it, and you will do amazing. Don't get frustrated. We have all been there. If we haven't, there wouldn't be millions of self-help books. Also, to reiterate, I cheat a lot.

MOST USED BREAKUP LINES

Don't ask me why I included these lines. I guess so you can know for sure they broke up with you. If you bought this book because you knew you were going to break up with your significant other and didn't know the right words to use? Here you go.

You are probably wondering, why would anyone buy this book if they were the breaker? It still hurts, and they needed the reassurance they are doing the right thing.

I am here to tell you if you are having doubts, then yes, it is time to end it. If they are the one, you guys will get back together. I have seen it with one of my friends. They let each other go, but everyone knew they were going to get back together.

- ❖ I think we should see other people.

- ❖ I do not want to be in a relationship right now.

- ❖ We are in totally different places in our lives.

- ❖ I need some space.

- ❖ I need to find myself again.

THE Breakup BAND AID

- I have no time for a relationship.

- This is not working for me.

- I need to work on myself. I cannot be in love with you if I do not love myself.

- I love you, but I love me more.

- It's not you, it's me.

- It's not me, it's you.

- I'm sorry, but this isn't working.

- I need some space and time to find myself.

- We're better off as friends.

- I didn't know what I wanted out of a relationship but this is not it.

- I was the one who pursued you, now it's time for me to leave.

- I think we need to think about where we are going.

- Our love came at the wrong time.

- This is the hardest thing I've ever had to do, but…

- Something tells me we aren't right for each other.

- Remember the other day when I said we would be together forever? Well, things changed and I found someone else.

- In this time of our lives we should be happy. We're both miserable and we both know why.

- ❖ You are such a great person and such a great friend. I don't want to break your heart, but…

- ❖ We have to end this before we end up hating each other.

- ❖ When we met and were together it was great, but now…

- ❖ Remember when we used to smile? I really miss that.

- ❖ Did I tell you lately how much I appreciate you? I realize now I can't keep taking advantage of you and I have to end this.

- ❖ Sometimes people change.

- ❖ Sometimes our dreams and paths change and ours aren't on the same route anymore.

- ❖ I don't know why, but this doesn't feel right anymore.

- ❖ I love you, but this is a bad time for us to be together.

- ❖ We rushed into this relationship too fast.

- ❖ There is no right time to say this, so I'm just going to do it.

- ❖ Maybe if we met at a different time.

- ❖ Are you feeling the same way I am, but are too afraid to admit it?

- ❖ I'd like to ask you a question. Do you still feel the same about us as you once did? Honestly, I don't.

- ❖ We really should discuss our relationship before we end up hating each other. It's time we said goodbye.

- ❖ I don't want to hurt you, but…

- ❖ I am sorry, but this isn't right for either of us.

THE Breakup BAND AID

- I have to say this before I lose my nerve. This relationship isn't healthy for either of us, and we need to talk about it.

- We've outgrown each other.

- I'm going in a different direction.

- I've changed.

- I'm not the person you once knew.

- You suck.

- I suck.

- I don't want to live a lie.

- The pressure has gotten to me.

- What's monogamy good for anyway?

- There is no passion anymore.

- I've been faking orgasms for a while.

- I haven't fallen for you yet, and I feel like I should have already.

- I can't deal with your drama anymore, Sarah!

- Maybe if you weren't so crazy, Sarah!

- I want to move to California, and you want to die a mile from where you were born.

- I did a genealogy test, and it came back. We're fifteenth cousins.

- I have a New Year's resolution and it's to get rid of excess baggage.

SARAH MELLAND

- ❖ You are starting to bore me.

- ❖ I hate your family.

- ❖ I am allergic to you.

COMEBACKS FOR WHEN YOUR EX SAYS IT'S OVER

Duh! Why wouldn't I have comebacks in here? It's like the most important thing for when they say, "Sayonara, Sissy." You should memorize your favorites out of this list for your next breakup or when you are blindsided and have nothing prepared. As always, you are welcome.

- ❖ Oh well, every happy woman has at least one ex-boyfriend behind them.

- ❖ Ok. (Don't say anything more. They made their decision. Don't try to convince them otherwise, it doesn't work. Walk out and don't turn back.)

- ❖ Yeah, I see you as more of a brother/father figure.

- ❖ Yeah, I see you as more of a sister/mother figure.

- ❖ That's alright. I love you, but I'm not in love with you.

- ❖ That's okay, I know I'm not your type. I'm not inflatable!

- ❖ It's okay, I actually agree things were getting a little stale and I wanted to experiment a bit.

- ❖ There didn't seem to be any passion in the bedroom. I had to fake it every time we had sex, and I shouldn't have to do that.

- ❖ I think I've been guilty of romanticizing this whole thing. You're not really everything I thought you were. I was putting you on a pedestal. My therapist said I should stop doing that.

- ❖ Cool. When you see me with someone else, don't you dare come running back to me.

- ❖ That's OK. Lately, I've been feeling like I'm too gorgeous to be with someone like you!

- ❖ Thanks, because I fell out of love with you ages ago and just didn't know how to tell you. I'm not good with breakups, I always want to be the dumpee so I wouldn't hurt your feelings.

- ❖ Oh, that's a relief because I've fallen in love with someone else.

- ❖ Is it OK if I date your best friend/boss/brother/father?

- ❖ Is it OK if I date your sister/mother?

- ❖ That's OK. I've been cheating on you for months.

- ❖ I have to admit, I've been seeing someone else. How did you know?

- ❖ Let's bury this relationship and be done with it.

- ❖ I can't stand another day being around you.

- ❖ Fine, I haven't been honest with you during our entire relationship.

THE Breakup BAND AID

- Oh. Poor me! How will I survive? Bye.

- I know! I was getting kind of bored dating you.

- Well we were going to split over religious differences sooner or later, with you thinking you're God and me disagreeing.

- All I can say is thank you for being the one to show me what kind of person I don't want to be with.

- You must have been reading my mind. I've wanted out of this crappy relationship with you for weeks now!

- OK, I've got places to go, things to see and people to do!

- Oh, thank goodness! Now I don't have to pretend I've been happy in our relationship!

- That's OK. It only takes one bad boyfriend to make you realize you deserve so much better!

- I can't stand the sight of your body naked.

- Ummmm...This is awkward, I was just about to dump you!

- I'm looking for someone a little more intelligent.

- If you're stupid enough to walk away, then I'm smart enough to let you go.

- K. Thanks. Bye.

- I hated the way you touched my vagina.

- I hated the way you sucked my dick.

- Works for me.

SARAH MELLAND

❖ Your breath smelled bad and I was always too afraid to tell you. Well, now since it's over, I thought it's best you know, so you can fix that before your next relationship.

❖ Your penis is crooked and oddly shaped. You should probably get that checked out and make sure it is OK. I didn't want to say anything at first, but now…

❖ I can't date a guy who still lives with his mommy.

❖ You have womanly hands.

HOW TO MAKE YOUR EX JEALOUS

I think this section needs no introduction. Enjoy! Get pumped, you look phenomenal!

❖ Do not stop working, exercising and hanging out with friends. This is a breakup, not the end of the world. I promise it will get better. I survived it. Multiple times. The first was the hardest. Second, was annoying. Third, got cheated on with a porn star. Fourth, had bad breath and I cringe now thinking that I allowed him to touch me. Hey, we all make mistakes, or are desperate and don't want to be alone. (See the Marilyn Monroe quote.) I will not be dating men when I am desperate. I will only date when I am content and happy. When you give off desperate vibes, you get it back.

❖ Please for the love of God, do not post dramatic or sad Facebook posts airing your dirty laundry. Also, do not Instagram sappy sad breakup sayings. Don't Snapchat you crying with a kitten filter! I swear, I will fly out to your state and slap you! Post happy fun pics. Don't do staged though, it screams desperate.

- You always want to look good after a breakup. You might find your future husband or run into your ex. Either way don't look sloppy and disheveled.

- If you run into your ex, be casual. Say stupid shit like "Boy, the weather sure is nice…" I hate when people say that to me, it's such an annoying conversation filler. Don't look sad. How are you? Good? You? Perfect. The End. Bu-Bye.

- Don't comment if they look different or exceptional. Be nice. Don't act like a stalker when you hear your song playing in the background. Act like it doesn't faze you. True story. Have to admit the timing couldn't have been more perfectly awkward.

- Always act like you are in a hurry and have places to be. You don't need to catch up with them.

- Don't ever be mean or a jerk to your ex. Please act like you don't care and are happy for them. If you act like a bitch, it's not attractive. They will get a weird feeling from you and be glad they broke up with you.

- Be so confident you illuminate the room with your presence.

- Pretend not to see them if there is an accidental run-in at the grocery store.

I will let you start dating now. We are almost done. I feel you have learned a lot. You know how to conquer anything life throws at you about a breakup. Go get 'em tiger!

MORE DUMB BREAKUP STORIES SO YOU DON'T HAVE TO...

MY BIRTHDAY

Ahh. My 21st birthday. To be 21 again. To be able to drink shot after shot after shot, drink after drink, and be able to wake up the next morning feeling perfect. This is not a story about being perfect. I wish I were perfect. I wouldn't have been so stupid.

What happened on my 21st birthday wasn't important. I got drunk. I had a lot of shots. I don't remember if I did anything stupid at the bar. I think I was pretty well-behaved. I had shots I could handle and drinks which had low alcohol content. My favorite was Tequila Rose and Mountain Dew. It sounds terrible but trust me it tasted like strawberry milkshake goodness.

Around four a.m. I was still up and knew he would be getting off work. I called and called him until he picked up. I told him I was coming over. He told me I would be sleeping on the couch if I did. The only reason he answered was because I told him I couldn't find my keys and couldn't get in my house. He knew it was a lie and told me to stay at my friend Lauren's. I was persistent. I could tell he was getting upset with me. My dumbass thought he would see me and have sex with me because it was my birthday. I was wrong.

In the era before Uber and Lyft, there were taxis, and they sucked. I decided I would walk from 11th street to 1st street in heels. I feel like I also ran part of it. Whatever I did, it was stupid. I think I was just making sure he wasn't bringing home a slutty container who liked her salad tossed. I knew what I had made him into. Before me, he wasn't getting hot chicks. He was barely getting chicks. I turned that asshole into an Adonis, and he should be forever grateful.

Anyhooters, he let me in, but I had to spend the night on an awful futon where you can feel every bar. Not a pleasant futon, an old college futon, probably the first futon ever invented. I woke up early and couldn't believe what a loser I had become. I was a fucking loser. I snuck out and walked home. I didn't even say goodbye.

Instead of going out a second night, which most 21-year-olds would do, I drove down to Milwaukee to see my girlfriend and take a good look at my life. I was never going to get over him if I kept going out and seeing him every night.

I decided I was going to stay away for at least a month. I couldn't see him. It hurt too much, and I was literally going crazy. Who is this girl? She used to be happy and carefree. She will get out sometime. She's in there, I know it.

HALLOWEEN

I'm going to make this one short and sweet because these unbearable stories are hurting my thirty-year-old soul.

I was dressed up as Marilyn Monroe. I saw him as I went to the first bar on our rounds that night. He was walking to his bar to start his shift. He gave me some compliment like I looked stunning. It was also the beginning of the night, so I wasn't drunk yet.

Marilyn turned into a not pretty sight. I met up with some old high school friends and got wasted, like disgustingly wasted. No Marilyn should ever do that. Wasted. I was puking in the bathroom and couldn't even stand up anymore. I had to be carried out of the bar by a sexy barmaid and a naughty nurse. When I say carried, I mean carried. Please don't ever be this disgusting. It is not pretty or attractive. Why would your sober ex ever want to take care of disgusting you? Don't worry. I didn't call him that night…I don't think? I mean let's face it, I probably did.

THE *Breakup* BAND AID

GOING AWAY PARTY

When I was moving to California I kept emailing him asking if he wanted me to stay. I would unfollow my dreams and stay in this shitty town for him. Am I fucking nuts? Why in the hell would I have ever thought that would work? I would have had to spend my miserable life here. Something I didn't want to do. I'd still be working at Wal-Mart and move into the management program instead of being the most influential female writer of our time like I wanted to be.

I've always wanted to be a writer ever since I can remember. I always wanted to move to Hollywood. Even at a young age, it was in my blood. I knew I was destined to be a writer and I was still willing to give all of that up for some guy who was unhappy with his life? I mean, really Sarah? You could go to LA and find hundreds of him. (No comment, but that's what I thought.)

You have to get to a point in your life where you say fuck it, I need to be happy, and he is never coming back to me. I made one last-ditch attempt, created an event on Facebook and invited him. He works every Saturday. I mean EVERY Saturday. Amazingly my going away party Saturday, he had off and was drinking as if to say "I'm sending you mixed signals, but I don't want you back." That's exactly what he was doing. He told me good luck in the shittiest way. In the "you will never make it out there, and you will be back in six months" way.

I tried to have sex with that idiot one more time, and it didn't work. Duh... does it ever? End of story. I moved to LA and didn't look back.

FB MESSAGE FROM HIS EX/CHRISTMAS PARTY

All the time I was trying to get over the idiot, I was dating this dude as a filler for the time being. He was getting over a long-term relationship, and so was I. We weren't looking for anything serious, but we were starting to fall for each other.

Until I found out on Facebook that he spent the night at his ex's house. I put two and two together with what my roommate told me and what I saw on her wall posted by his friend. I was mad at him, but

I couldn't be too mad. After all, I was still trying to get back together with my ex.

The next night he came up to me and apologized. I was trying to act cool like it didn't bother me. That night, I also had the pleasure of meeting his ex-girlfriend who was out for the first time. Her friend played cool and acted like we were friends as we have a class together. That's when I was ambushed. She puts forward her hand and is like "I'm so and so. Step off!" I rolled my eyes and didn't care. I smirked at her and couldn't believe how much weight she had gained since I stalked her last on social media.

When I woke up in the morning, I had drunken Facebook messages from her. Telling me she could smell the desperation on my shirt, and a bunch of other nonsensical drunk jibber jabber. The next semester we had an uncomfortable class together. We both weren't dating him anymore, but we both still hated each other.

Funny story; two years later I moved to LA. Four years later, I am at this random Christmas party with my girlfriends in Santa Monica when I hear this voice say "Kara?" I was like, "No, I am Sarah." I had no idea who this girl was. She kept telling me I looked familiar. I could not place her for the life of me. I thought she might be one of my clients because she looked tan. After about ten minutes she finally placed me. She told me her name, and I was like, "Shit!" She said in a scared voice, "We're OK, right?" We laughed and joked about him and couldn't believe he got married.

I guess the moral of the story is two ex-girlfriends can be friends... sort of. I don't ever remember talking to her after that but we were OK.

WHEN I WENT BACK TO A CHEATER

This is a tale of desperation. When I say desperation, I mean desperate. I was so over dating. I was exhausted. The porn star porker popped back up in my life and I thought why not. He said he never cheated and he promised it happened after me. I wanted this to work, so I just dropped it.

There were red flags right away; girls texting him at 12:30 in the morning to be specific. (Don't be that type of girl. If you want to know the whole story, please read my upcoming book *Romances of a SAIF in*

LA. This amazing masterpiece of a book also follows my journey as to how I play men like they play women. If we do this together, men will start treating us the way we want to be treated. Are guys seriously reading this book?)

He kept a distance but kept telling me what I wanted to hear. I got fed up and realized he hadn't changed. He cheated on me because he needed constant attention from women to feel validated.

This story is short and sweet. Don't ever go back to a cheater. It's not worth your time. Trust me. I did it, so you don't have to. Again, you are welcome.

WHEN CLOSURE ISN'T ENOUGH, BUT ENOUGH

I went back home and contacted Eric because I was sick of all the men in LA. I thought maybe he would move out here. He was the best man I knew. He treated me like a queen. No guys in LA that I have ever dated have treated me even close to how he did.

To my surprise, he was willing to meet up and ready to travel to see me. We set up a time to watch the Packers game together. We had a great time catching up, and I got a wee bit drunk. Not a bad drunk, but a good enough drunk so I would be able to talk to him.

He wasn't the same man I had dated. His outlook on life had changed. He didn't want to date women. He didn't care.

After the meeting, we hugged each other. When I got back to my girlfriend's house, I started crying, not because I wanted him back and couldn't get him. I wanted him to be happy, and he wasn't happy. He was miserable. It was awful. For the first time in my life, I finally knew I was over him. I wanted him to find a beautiful girl and be happy.

He started texting me. For the first time since we broke up. Meaning: he texted me first. I wanted to clarify. He was texting me saying how we should meet up more often and not wait six years. For the first time since we broke up, I didn't want him back. I knew I finally had the closure I needed. We were not in the same place anymore. We had been young kids, and now we were grown adults.

He tried. He said, "Goodbye doesn't mean forever." I said, "What does that mean?" That's when he stopped. And I was OK.

THERE SHOULD BE AN APP FOR THAT...

By the time this book comes out, I am bound and determined to develop an app for when you enter your ex's name, it blocks both of you from seeing anything about each other on all social media. Plus, you won't be able to google, email, call or text each other. Everything you can possibly imagine. Also, I would get rid of pesky telemarketers and block them too. Once again, you are welcome!

UPDATE: Can't do it, too expensive. Apparently, it's like $100,000 for a good app device to be developed, and then you have to update it every time the system updates and that costs even more money. So, if anybody can do it for cheap, you are welcome for my billion-dollar idea.

GIVING BACK

I will be donating 10% of my book sales to Leslie's Helping Hands. I had the privilege of meeting the founder, Penny Waldroup, last year. I have been writing this book for over ten years... not really. I sat on it for five years because I was scared. Scared of what? I don't know. Conquer your fears!

I always knew I wanted to donate part of my book sales to a domestic violence shelter. I didn't know which one and also wanted to make sure the proceeds went for good, not to overpaid employees.

As a child growing up with domestic violence, only to repeat the cycle in her adulthood, Penny finds it essential for communities to become educated on the impact of domestic violence on the children who grow up in these circumstances. Penny's goal is to teach our youth about boundaries, healthy dating relationships, as well as provide education to adults who are currently in an unhealthy domestic situation.

She also helps rebuild homes for domestic violence victims. Such as obtaining personal items like clothing, shoes, furniture, house accessories, groceries, cleaning supplies, etc. Too often when one flees from their abuser, they leave with just the clothing on their back.

REFERENCES

Jynx. "7 Best Celebrity Broken Heart Quotes." Yes, We're Jynx. 3 December 2009. http://jynx7.blogspot.com/2009/12/7-best-celebrity-broken-heart-quotes.html

Corbano, Eddie. "10 Positive Break Up Quotes And What We Can Learn From Them." Loves a Game. 7 June 2017. http://lovesagame.com/10-positive-break-up-quotes-and-what-we-can-learn-from-them/breakup-songs.com/

Twenty-five. "Best Break Up Quotes and Sayings." Hub Pages. 14 June 2012. http://twentyfive.hubpages.com/hub/Best-Break-up-Quotes-and-Sayings

"Inspiring Quotes for a Depressed Heart." Beliefnet. http://www.beliefnet.com/Health/Emotional-Health/Depression/10-Inspiring-Quotes-for-a-Depressed-Heart.aspx?p=4#ixzz1jIy4UxjQ

Strictly Dating. "Awesome, Terrible, Funny and Nasty Things to Say if Your Boyfriend Dumps You." Hub Pages. 9 March 2019. http://strictlydating.hubpages.com/hub/What-To-Say-When-Hes-Dumped-You-To-Hit-Him-Where-It-Hurst-Most

Ayyar, A. "How to Make Your Ex Jealous – Tips and Advice." Future Scopes.
http://www.futurescopes.com/breaking/763/how-make-your-ex-boyfriend-jealous-tips-and-advice

BECAUSE YOU KNOW HOW MUCH I LOVE SOCIAL MEDIA...

What book wouldn't be complete without one final plug to follow the author on social media?

Facebook: @youdatingunexpert
Instagram: @yourdatingunexpert

Instagram: @ohmymelons
Twitter: @ohmymelons
Snapchat: @ohmymelons (I never check this, so don't bother.)

Website: www.sarahmelland.com